SECOND-CENTURY CHRISTIANITY

SECOND-CENTURY CHRISTIANITY

A Collection of Fragments

Second Edition

Robert M. Grant

Westminster John Knox Press
LOUISVILLE • LONDON

Book design by Sharon Adams
Cover design by Mark Abrams
Cover photograph of second-century stone tablet
  © *Sandro Vannini/CORBIS*

Second edition
Published by Westminster John Knox Press
Louisville, Kentucky

This book is printed on acid-free paper that meets the American National Standards Institute Z39.48 standard. ∞

PRINTED IN THE UNITED STATES OF AMERICA

03 04 05 06 07 08 09 10 11 12 — 10 9 8 7 6 5 4 3 2 1

Library of Congress Cataloging-in-Publication Data

Second-century Christianity : a collection of fragments / [compiled]
  by Robert M. Grant.—New ed.
      p. cm.
  Includes bibliographical references (p.) and index.
  ISBN 0-664-22638-8 (alk. paper)
  1. Christian literature, Early.   2. Christianity—Early works to 1800.
  I. Grant, Robert McQueen, 1917–

  BR63.S43 2003
  270.1—dc21   2003043083

Contents

Part I

Pagan Witnesses

*T*estimonies to early Christianity by outsiders come from ten Roman and Greek authors of the second century. First there was the popular Stoic philosopher Epictetus, disciple of Musonius Rufus; both men were greatly admired by many early Christians. Others include emperors and Roman officials who were acquaintances and shared similar "official" views of the new religion. Pliny the Younger was governor of Bithynia and Pontus on the Black Sea around 110. He reported to the emperor Trajan (98–117) and received instructions from him. The historian Tacitus was proconsul of Asia under Trajan, and Suetonius was a secretary to Trajan's successor Hadrian, emperor from 117 to 138. Then comes Fronto, who taught rhetoric to Marcus Aurelius and was consul in 140 and again in 145. Later in the century we meet the emperor Marcus Aurelius, the satirist Lucian, and the physician-author and imperial favorite Galen.

1
EPICTETUS

Epictetus was an ex-slave who became a Stoic teacher and, after being banished from Rome under Domitian, at the end of the first century, conducted a school at Nicopolis in Asia. There his pupil, the Roman administrator Arrian, had his lectures and conversations recorded. He refers clearly to the Christians only once, calling them "Galileans."

If madness can produce this attitude [of detachment] toward these things [death, loss of family and property], and also habit, as with the Galileans,

3

can no one learn from reason and demonstration that God has made everything in the universe, and the whole universe itself, to be unhampered and
self-sufficient, and the parts of it for the use of the whole?[1]

2
PLINY THE YOUNGER[2]

As legate of the emperor Trajan to Pontus-Bithynia on the southern
shore of the Black Sea, the Roman equestrian Pliny was sent out to
provide "law and order," especially fiscal, in this distant province
close to the eastern frontier of the empire. He was unsure what to do
about the fairly obscure sect known as Christians and therefore asked
Trajan how to proceed against them.

It is my custom, Majesty, to refer to you everything about which I have
doubts. For who can better check my hesitation or inform my ignorance?
I have never attended examinations of Christians, and therefore I do not
know what and how far it is customary to investigate or to punish. And I
felt considerable hesitation as to whether age should be taken into consid-
eration or whether the weak should be differentiated from the stronger,
whether pardon should follow repentance or whether one who had completely abandoned Christianity should benefit, and whether the name itself,
absent crimes, or the crimes inherent in the name should be punished.

Meanwhile I have followed this procedure in the case of those who were
denounced to me as Christians. I asked them if they were Christians. If
they confessed, I asked a second and third time, threatening with punishment: I ordered those who persevered to be led away. For I did not doubt
that whatever it might be that they confessed, certainly their stubbornness
and unshakeable obstinacy ought to be punished. There were others of a
like madness who were Roman citizens, and I took note of their names for
sending to the city [for trial].

Presently because of the existence of the investigation, as often hap-
pens, the accusation became widespread and more cases came up. An
anonymous pamphlet was handed in with the names of many persons. I
thought I should release those who denied that they were or had been
Christians, when following my lead they first invoked the gods and offered
incense and wine to your image, which for this purpose I had ordered
brought in with the images of the gods, and afterwards cursed Christ. It is

said that those who are really Christians cannot be forced to do any of these things. Others named in the indictment said they were Christians but presently denied it; they had been Christians but had stopped, some two years, others many years ago, a few twenty years past.[3] All of them reverenced your image and the images of the gods and cursed Christ. They testified that this was the whole of their crime or error, that they had met regularly before dawn on a fixed day and recited an antiphonal ode to Christ as to a god, and took an oath not for committing any crime but instead for not committing thefts, robberies, or adulteries, nor to refuse to repay a deposit. They had even stopped doing this after my edict, by which in accordance with your commission I had forbidden associations to exist.

I believed it all the more necessary to find out the truth from two slave women, whom they call deaconesses, even by torture. I found nothing but depraved and immoderate superstition. Therefore suspending the investigation I hastened to consult you. It seems to me a matter worthy of consultation, especially because of the number endangered. For many of every age and every rank and even of both sexes are called into danger and will be called. The contagion of this superstition was spread not only through towns but also villages and even rural areas. Certainly it is clear enough that temples long deserted are beginning to be filled and sacred rites long lapsed are resuming, along with the sale of sacrificial victims, for which rather recently there were only occasional buyers. From this it is easy to conclude that the mass of mankind can be reformed if an opportunity is given to repent.

3
THE EMPEROR TRAJAN

Trajan replies to the letter of Pliny just cited, approving his procedure, though without mentioning the use of his own statue.

You have followed the right procedure, my Secundus, in examining the cases of those who had been reported to you as Christians, for it is impossible to set forth any universal rule with a fixed form. They are not to be searched for. If they are reported and convicted they must be punished, but if someone denies he is a Christian and proves it by offering prayers to our gods, he is to obtain pardon by his repentance, even though he was previously suspect. Anonymous pamphlets, however, must have no place in any accusation. They follow the worst precedent and do not belong to our age.[4]

4
CORNELIUS TACITUS

Though Tacitus, proconsul of Asia probably in 112–113, said there was *quies* in Judaea under Tiberius,[5] he was referring to Jewish revolts, not to intra-Jewish movements like the earliest Christianity. He first discusses Christians when dealing with the fire at Rome under Nero.[6] He certainly does not admire the Christians, though he does not admire Nero either.

To obliterate the rumor [that he had started the fire] Nero substituted as guilty, and punished with the most refined tortures, a group hated for its crimes and called "Christians" by the mob. After Christus, the founder of the name, had been punished by death through the procurator Pontius Pilate, the hateful superstition was suppressed for a moment but burst forth again not only in Judaea, where this evil originated, but even in the City, where all things horrible and shameful flow together and are celebrated. First, then, those who confessed were arrested; then on their report a huge multitude was convicted not so much of the crime of arson as for their hatred of the human race. Public torments were added to their death. They were covered with the skins of wild beasts and torn to death by dogs, or they were fastened to crosses, and, when daylight failed, burned to serve as light by night. Nero had offered his gardens for the spectacle and provided a circus show, mingling with the crowd in the dress of a charioteer or mounted on his chariot. Hence compassion arose toward them (though they were guilty and deserved the most extreme punishment) as being sacrificed not for the public welfare but for the savagery of one man.[7]

5
SUETONIUS

Suetonius was a friend and protegé of Pliny the Younger and may have gone with him to Bithynia around 111. Ten years later he was

Hadrian's secretary *ab epistulis* and at work on his *Lives of the Twelve Caesars* when the emperor dismissed him.

1. Since the Jews were constantly rioting under the leadership of Chrestus, he [Claudius] expelled them from Rome.[8]

It is not clear whether or not Suetonius has in mind "Christ," a name sometimes spelled "Chrestus," or some Jewish leader.

2. [Under Nero] punishments were inflicted on the Christians, a group of men with a new and harmful superstition.[9]

6
THE EMPEROR HADRIAN

The recipient of this letter was proconsul of Asia in 122–123, when Christians were victims of mob actions. Hadrian urged him to investigate before taking any action. Later on, Melito of Sardis (see chapter 18) mentioned this letter.

To Minucius Fundanus. I have received a letter written to me from your predecessor, the most illustrious Serennius Granianus. It seems to me that the matter should not remain without investigation, so that men may not be troubled or provide subject-matter for the malice of informers. If then the provincials can make a strong case for this petition against the Christians, so that they can answer for it before the court, they will turn to this alone, not to petitions or outcries. For it is much more suitable, if anyone wants to bring charges, for you to examine this point. If then anyone accuses them and shows that they are acting against the laws, make your decision according to the nature of the offence; but by Hercules, if anyone brings the matter forward for the sake of blackmail, investigate with severity and take care to exact retribution.[10]

7
CORNELIUS FRONTO

The famous orator Fronto was tutor in Latin rhetoric to the young Marcus Aurelius and Lucius Verus after 136 and became suffect consul in

143, only a few years before Marcus abandoned rhetoric for philosophy. A fragment from Fronto against the Christians seems to be preserved in the *Octavius* of Minucius Felix, a Christian apologist of the second century. It includes a typical slander against Christian behavior.

On a regular day Christians of both sexes and every age meet for a feast with all their children, sisters, and mothers. Then after much feasting, when the banquet has heated up and the flame of impure lust and drunkenness has been lit, a dog tied to the lampstand is incited to jump and dance by a little cake tossed beyond the area of its tether. When the witnessing light is thus turned over and extinguished, the guests under cover of the shameless darkness embrace one another in their unspeakable lust as chance brings them together and, in guilt if not in fact, all alike are incestuous, since whatever can result by the act of individuals is potentially desired by the wish of all.[11]

Possibly, as Haines suggests, "the paragraph immediately preceding this in Minucius Felix, giving an equally unveracious description of the 'Thyestean banquets' attributed to the Christians, is similar in style to this extract, and probably came from the same source."[12] Though Minucius explicitly ascribes only "incestuous banquets," not cannibalistic ones, to Fronto's account (31.1–2), C. P. H. Bammel has argued for his more extensive use of Fronto ("Die erste lateinische Rede gegen die Christen," *Zeitschrift für Kirchengeschichte* 104 [1993]: 295–311).

8
THE EMPEROR MARCUS AURELIUS

The *Meditations* of the emperor Marcus Aurelius (161–180), perhaps copied from notebooks after his death, contain only one (critical) reference to the Christians.

How admirable is the soul which is ready, if it must already be released from the body, either to be extinguished or scattered, or to persist. This readiness must come from its own decision, not from mere opposition like the Christians, but rationally, religiously, and so as to persuade others, without dramatics.[13]

9
LUCIAN OF SAMOSATA

The satirist Lucian from Samosata in Syria composed many biting and amusing works during the second half of the second century. He was acquainted with the Christians, whom he depicts as foes of the fraud magician Alexander at Amastris in Pontus but as dupes of the grandiloquent Peregrinus Proteus, who immolated himself at Olympia in 167.

Alexander

1. When many intelligent men combined against him . . . he issued a proclamation to terrify them, stating that Pontus had been filled with atheists and Christians who ventured to express the worst blasphemies about him. He ordered his hearers to drive them away with stones if they wanted to have the god favor them.[14]

[At Abonuteichos] he established a mystery rite with torchlights and priestly offices to be held for three consecutive days. On the first day, as at Athens, there was this proclamation: "If any atheist or Christian or Epicurean has come to spy on the mysteries, let him flee, but those who believe the god must perform the rites with good fortune." Then at the start came an "expulsion," which Alexander led, saying, "Out with Christians," while the whole crowd replied, "Out with Epicureans."[15]

Peregrinus

2. He learned the wonderful wisdom of the Christians when he associated with their priests and scribes in Palestine. What else? He shortly made them like children [cf. Matt. 18:3], becoming their prophet and cult-leader and convener and everything else, all by himself. He interpreted and explained some of their books and composed many himself, and they considered him like a god, used him as a legislator, and noted him as a protector, next after that one whom they still worship—the man crucified in Palestine—because he introduced this new rite to human life.

Later Peregrinus was arrested for this and cast into prison, which itself gave him no insignificant reputation for the rest of his life and for the miracle-working and the search for the notoriety that he loved. When he was imprisoned, the Christians, viewing the event as a disaster, did everything they could to rescue him. Then, as this was impossible, they gave him every other form of attention, not casually but with zeal. Right at daybreak one could see aged widows and orphan children waiting by the prison, while their officers even slept inside it with him after bribing the guards. Then elaborate meals were brought in and their sacred discourses were read, and they called the most excellent Peregrinus (for he still went by that name) "the new Socrates."

Indeed, people even came from the cities of Asia, sent by the Christians at their common expense, to help and defend and encourage the man. They exhibit incredible speed whenever such public action is taken, for they swiftly spend everything. So much money then came to Peregrinus because of his imprisonment, and he obtained no small income.

The poor wretches have persuaded themselves that they will be immortal and will live forever, and consequently they despise death and most of them willingly give themselves up. Moreover their first legislator persuaded them that they are all brothers of one another, once they have transgressed by denying the Greek gods, by worshiping that crucified sophist himself, and by living according to his laws. They therefore despise all things equally and consider them common property and accept all their doctrines without accurate demonstration. So if any charlatan or trickster able to use opportunities comes to them, he quickly becomes rich by imposing on simple people.[16]

He [Peregrinus] left home for the second time, with the Christians as an adequate source of funds; through their gifts he enjoyed everything abundantly. For some time he was nurtured thus, but then, having transgressed even against them—for he was seen, I think, eating some food forbidden them—they no longer accepted him.[17]

10
GALEN[18]

Galen began studying philosophy at Pergamum in 143, when he was fourteen. He went on to anatomy three years later, and, after his father's death a year or so after that, proceeded to study medicine at Smyrna, Corinth, and Alexandria. He became physician to the gladiatorial school at Pergamum in 157 but after four years left for Rome, where he began his forty-year career as author and ultimately court physician to Marcus Aurelius, Commodus, and Septimius Severus. During the plague in Italy that broke out in 166, he withdrew to Pergamum, but Marcus Aurelius summoned him to Aquileia for the German expedition two years later. After the sudden death of the coemperor Verus the next year, Galen returned to Rome as physician to the boy Caesar Commodus and within a few years wrote some major treatises while practising medicine. After writing his last major treatise, *Therapeutic Method*, he catalogued his own works, and may have died in 199.

Galen was acquainted with Christianity and probably with Christians, mentioning their irrational insistence on divine power as well as their contempt of death, abstinence in sex and diet, and pursuit of justice. Marcus Aurelius, too, had noted their "readiness for death," but without enthusiasm. Under Commodus persecution was unusual, and around 190 his concubine Marcia was able to obtain the release of Christian prisoners on Sardinia.[19] If Galen knew about this event and was aware that Marcia later conspired against the emperor, his attitude toward Christians might well have become even more ambivalent. Later, as Galen busied himself with antidotes to the poisons Septimius Severus might ingest, the new emperor was protecting Christians of senatorial rank from the mob.[20] In any event there were links between the society of Galen and Roman Christians, links favoring the transmission of his critical ideas to them, not the reverse.

Galen ascribes three statements about undemonstrated tradition to disciples of both Moses and Christ, perhaps around 176–180,[21] while he differentiates Christians around 180. Though no philosophers, they despise death; exercise self-control in sex, food, and drink; and pursue justice.[22] Walzer compares Galen's admiration for uneducated slaves who in 185 underwent torture rather than betray their masters.[23] Even more important, Galen treats Christian behavior as resembling what he found in the "exhortations ascribed to Pythagoras," which he read twice a day; they favored not only Epicurean freedom from anger but also cleansing from gluttony, lechery, drunkenness, meddling, and envy.[24] Around this time Pythagorean moral dicta were also being ascribed to the Christian author Sextus.[25]

Fragments

1. They compare those who practise medicine without scientific knowledge to Moses, who framed laws for the tribe of the Jews, since it is his method in his books to write without offering proofs, saying "God commanded, God spake."[26]

2. For [Moses] it seems enough to say that God simply willed the arrangement of matter and it was presently arranged in due order; for he

believes everything to be possible with God, even should he wish to make a bull or a horse out of ashes. We however do not hold this. . . .[27]

3. One might more easily teach novelties to the followers of Moses and Christ than to the physicians and philosophers who cling fast to their schools.[28]

4. . . . in order that one should not at the very beginning, as if one had come into the school of Moses and Christ, hear talk of undemonstrated laws, and that where it is least appropriate.[29]

5. The followers of Moses and Christ order them [their pupils] to accept everything on faith. . . .[30]

6. Most people are unable to follow any demonstrative argument consecutively; hence they need parables, and benefit from them . . . just as now we see the people called Christians drawing their faith from parables and miracles and yet sometimes acting in the same way [as those who philosophize]. For they include not only men but also women who refrain from cohabiting all through their lives; and they also number individuals who, in self-discipline and self-control in matters of food and drink, and in their keen pursuit of justice, have attained a pitch not inferior to that of genuine philosophers.[31]

Part II

Christian Churches

The Church of Alexandria

11
JULIUS CASSIANUS

This author, probably Alexandrian, was cited by Clement of Alexandria, who calls him the originator of Docetism and claims that, like Tatian, he was a Valentinian. The one fragment does not confirm this notion, however.

Let us not say that since we have members such that one is female and another male, the one for receiving and the other for sowing, therefore sexual intercourse is from God. For if such an arrangement were from the God to whom we are hastening, he would not have called eunuchs blessed,[32] nor would the prophet have said they "were not a fruitless tree" [Isa. 56:3], turning from the tree to the man who of his own choice and purpose becomes a eunuch. . . . How wrongly, then, would one blame the Savior if he formed us and freed us from error and from the joining of the members and [mere] appendages[33] and genitals. . . . When Salome asked when the things of which he spoke would be known, the Lord said, "When you trample on the garment of shame and when the two become one and the male with the female neither male nor female."[34]

Clement comments thus: "We do not have this word in the four Gospels handed down to us, but in the Gospel of the Egyptians." (Compare 2 Clement 12.2: "The Lord himself, when asked by someone when his kingdom would appear, said, 'When the two are one and the outside is as the inside, and the male with the female neither male nor female.'"[35])

12
PANTAENUS

Pantaenus was a second-century Christian teacher at Alexandria before Clement. Practically nothing is known of what he taught. Origen notes that he himself imitated Pantaenus.

1. But as I [Origen] was devoted to the word, and the fame of our proficiency was spreading abroad, there approached me sometimes heretics, sometimes those conversant with Greek learning and especially philosophy, and I thought it right to examine the opinions of the heretics as well as the claim that philosophers make concerning truth. And in so doing we followed the example of Pantaenus, who before us was of assistance to many and had acquired no small attainments in these matters.[36]

2. "He set his tabernacle in the sun" [Ps. 19:4]. Some, like Hermogenes, say that the Savior himself set his body in the sun; others, [that it was in] the church of the faithful. But our Pantaenus said, "Usually prophecy makes indefinite statements and uses the present tense instead of the future, and again the present instead of the past."[37]

3. When the followers of Pantaenus were asked in what manner Christians suppose God to know reality, they replied, "He neither knows sensible things by sense nor intelligible things by intellect. For it is not possible that he who is above the things that exist should comprehend the things that exist in accordance with the things that exist. We say that he knows the things that exist as acts of his own will."[38]

The Church of Jerusalem

13
ARISTO OF PELLA

Dialogue of Jason and Papiscus

1. In this book a Christian is described as arguing with a Jew from the Jewish scriptures and showing that the prophecies about the Messiah refer to Jesus; and yet the adversary resists vigorously and in conformity with his Jewish character.[39]

2. "Accursed of God" is he who is hanged (Deut. 21:23).[40]

3. In the Son, God made heaven and earth.[41]

4. Seven heavens.[42]

5. The war was at its height in the eighteenth year of the reign [of Hadrian], round about Bethther, a small but very strong town not very far from Jerusalem, where a protracted siege brought the revolutionaries to complete destruction through hunger and thirst, and the author [Bar Cochba] of their folly paid the just penalty. From that time forward the entire nation was absolutely prohibited from setting foot upon the country round about Jerusalem, by the decree and ordinances of a law of Hadrian that forbade them to gaze, even from afar, on the land inherited from their fathers.[43]

14
HEGESIPPUS

The fragments of Hegesippus are focused on the church of Jerusalem, but he himself stood close to Rome. Eusebius gives a general picture. Hegesippus "states some particulars from the Gospel of the Hebrews and from the Syriac, and especially from the Hebrew language, showing [perhaps] that he himself was a convert from the Hebrews. He also records other matters as taken from the unwritten tradition of the Jews. And not only he but also Irenaeus and the whole chorus of the ancients called the Proverbs of Solomon 'all-virtuous Wisdom.' And in speaking of the so-called apocryphal books he tells us that some of them were forged in his own times by some of the sectarians."[44]

1. The various opinions in the circumcision among the sons of the Israelites against the tribe of Judah and the Messiah were these: Essenes, Galileans, Hemerobaptists, Masbotheans, Samaritans, Sadducees, and Pharisees.[45]

2. James the Lord's brother received the succession with the apostles in the church. He was called the Just by everyone from the Lord's times up to our own, since many were called James. But he was holy from his mother's womb; he did not drink wine or fermented drink, nor did he eat anything in which was life. No razor passed over his head [1 Sam. 1:11], he never anointed himself with oil, and he did not use the bath. It was lawful for him alone to enter into the Holy of Holies, for he did not wear wool but linen. He entered the temple alone, and was found kneeling on his knees and seeking forgiveness for the people, so that his knees grew hard as a camel's [because he was always kneeling on them, worshiping God and asking forgiveness for the people]. Because of the greatness of his righteousness he was called Just and Oblias[46] (in Greek that is Bulwark of the People and Righteousness), as the prophets foretold of him.

Then certain of the seven aforementioned sects among the people asked him, "What is the door[47] of Jesus?" And he said, "That he is Savior." The aforementioned sects do not believe either in [his] resurrection or that he will come to reward each in accordance with his works; but as many as believed did so on James's account. Then when many of the rulers also believed[48] there was a disturbance of the Jews and scribes and Pharisees, saying that the whole people is in danger of expecting Jesus as Messiah. Then coming to James they said, "We urge you to restrain the people, since they are led astray to Jesus as if he were the Messiah. We urge you to persuade about Jesus all who come for the day of Passover, for we all trust you. We and all the people bear witness to you that you are just and not a respecter of persons.[49] Therefore persuade the crowd not to be led astray concerning Jesus; for we and all the people trust you. Stand on the pinnacle of the temple so that you can be seen on high and your words can be clearly audible to the whole people. For all the tribes have come because of the Passover, and the gentiles too."

Then the aforementioned scribes and Pharisees set James on the pinnacle of the temple and shouted to him and said, "Just One, we all ought to trust you. Since the people are being led astray after Jesus the crucified, tell us what the door[50] of Jesus is." And he answered in a loud voice, "Why do you ask me about the Son of Man, when he sits in heaven at the right hand of the Great Power and is coming on the clouds of heaven?"

When many were persuaded, and gloried in the testimony of James, and said, "Hosanna to the Son of David," then again the same scribes and Pharisees said to one another, "We did wrong in allowing such a testimony to Jesus; but let us go up and throw him down so that they will be afraid to believe in him." And they shouted, "Oh, oh! The Just himself is deceived." And they fulfilled the scripture written in Isaiah [3:10]: "Let us take away the Just, for he is offensive to us; wherefore they shall eat the fruits of their doings." Then they went up and threw the Just One down and said to one another, "Let us stone James the Just," and they began to stone him since when thrown down he did not die but turned and knelt and said, "I exhort thee, Lord God Father, forgive them, for they know not what they do" [Luke 23:34]. As they were thus stoning him, one of the priests of the sons of Rechab the son of Rechabim (attested by the prophet Jeremiah [c. 35]) cried out saying, "Stop; what are you doing? The Just is praying for you." And one of them, a fuller, took a club which he used to beat clothes and smashed it against the head of the Just, and so he bore witness. And they buried him on the spot by the temple, and there his monument still lies, by the temple. He became a witness both to Jews and to Greeks that Jesus is the Messiah. And Vespasian immediately attacked them.[51]

3. And after James the Just was martyred as the Lord was, for the same offense, Simeon son of Clopas the Lord's uncle was appointed as the second bishop, a man whom everyone approved of, since he was a cousin of the Lord. They called the church a virgin for the reason that she had not yet been corrupted by vain discourses. But Thebouthis, because he had not become bishop, began to corrupt her from the seven sects among the people, to which he himself belonged. From these also came Simon, whence the Simonians, and Cleobius, whence the Cleobians, and Dositheus, whence the Dositheans, and Gorthaeus, whence the Gorathenes [and Masbotheans]. From these the Menandrianists and Marcionites and Carpocratians and Valentinians and Basilidians and Saturnilians have introduced their own opinions in various ways; from these have come false Christs,

false prophets, false apostles, who have divided the unity of the church with corrupting words against God and against his Christ.[52]

4. Some of these sectarians accused Simeon, the son of Clopas, of being a descendant of David and a Christian; and so he was martyred under Trajan and the legate Atticus at the age of 120.[53]

5. They came and ruled in the whole Church as witnesses and relatives of the Lord and, since there was profound peace in the whole Church, they survived until the emperor Trajan, until the son of an uncle of the Lord, the aforementioned Simeon son of Clopas, falsely accused by the sects, was similarly accused on the same charge before the legate Atticus. And after being tortured many days he bore witness, so that all were amazed, even the legate, at how he endured when he was 120 years old. Finally he was ordered off to be crucified.[54]

6. [Hegesippus] adds that the "Church continued until then as a pure and incorrupt virgin." Eusebius comments thus: "If there were any who tried to corrupt the sound doctrine of the preaching of salvation, they still hid in a dark hiding place. But when the sacred chorus of the apostles departed from life in various ways, as well as the generation of those who were deemed worthy to hear their inspired wisdom, then also the faction of godless error arose by the deceit of teachers of heterodoxy. These, since none of the apostles survived, henceforth shamelessly attempted to preach their 'knowledge falsely so-called' [1 Tim. 6:20] against the preaching of the truth."[55]

7. From the Lord's family the grandsons of Judas, called his brother after the flesh, were still living, and these were informed against as belonging to the family of David. The officer brought them to Domitian Caesar, who feared the coming of Christ as did Herod. He asked them if they belonged to David's family and they admitted it. Then he asked them what possessions they had or how much money they owned. They said that between them they had 9000 denarii, half belonging to each, and this, they said, was not in silver but in the value of only 39 *plethra* of land, on which they paid taxes and supported themselves by their labor. Then they showed him their hands to prove the hardness of their bodies, while the callouses on their hands formed by incessant work proved their labor.

And when they were asked about the Christ and his kingdom they replied that it was not worldly or earthly but heavenly and angelic to appear at the end of the age when he would come in glory to judge the living and the dead and to give to each according to his merits. For these remarks Domitian did not condemn them but, despising them as fools, sent them away free and by a decree stopped the persecution of the Church.

After they were set free they governed the churches both as witnesses and as relatives of the Lord. And since there was peace, they survived until the reign of Trajan.[56]

8. To whom they [idol-makers] have erected cenotaphs and temples to this day. Among them was Antinous, the slave of the emperor Hadrian, in whose honor games are celebrated; he lived in our own times. Hadrian also founded a city named after Antinous and instituted prophets.[57]

9. [After some observations on the epistle of Clement to the Corinthians] And the church of Corinth remained in the true faith until Primus was bishop in Corinth. I lived with them on my way to Rome and stayed with them for many days during which we were refreshed with the true teaching. And when I was in Rome I made a succession[58] up to Anicetus; Eleutherus was his deacon, Soter succeeded Anicetus, and after him came Eleutherus. In each succession and in each city things are done just as the Law, the prophets, and the Lord preach.[59]

10. "The good things prepared for the just, eye saw not and ear heard not, nor did they enter the heart of man" [1 Cor. 2:9]. Such a statement was made in vain, and those who made it lied against the divine scriptures and the Lord, who said, "Blessed are your eyes which see and your ears which hear," etc. [Matt. 13:16].[60]

The Church of Antioch

15
SERAPION OF ANTIOCH

Eusebius has a list of the early bishops at Antioch that includes Evodius, Ignatius (3.22), Hero, Cornelius, Eros, Theophilus (4.20), Maximinus (4.24), Serapion (5.22), and Asclepiades (6.11.4–12.6). Most are merely names, but Ignatius, Theophilus, and Serapion are exceptions because of their writings. Perhaps about 185–190 Serapion attacked the "new prophecy" of Montanism in a letter to Caricus and Pontius, men otherwise unknown.

1. "But that you may also know this, that the work of this lying party of the so-called New Prophecy is abominated by the whole brotherhood in the world, I have sent you also a letter of Claudius Apollinaris, who was the most blessed bishop in Hierapolis in Asia."[61]

He also opposed the docetic heresy maintained by some Christians at Rhosus near Antioch and apparently based on the apocryphal *Gospel of Peter*.

2. We, brothers, receive both Peter and the other apostles as Christ, but we reject the writings that falsely go under their names, since we are experienced and know that such were not handed down to us. For when I was among you [at Rhosus near Antioch] I supposed that all of you held to the true faith, and not having gone through the Gospel presented by them under the name of Peter, I said: If this is the only thing that seems to cause faultfinding among you, let it be read. But since I have now learned from what has been told me that their mind was enveloped in some heresy, I will

make haste to come to you again: therefore, brothers, expect me shortly. But we, brothers, understanding to what heresy Marcianus belonged (who used to contradict himself, not knowing what he said, as you will learn from what has been written to you), were enabled by others who studied this same Gospel, that is, by the successors of those who began it, whom we call Docetists (for most of the ideas belong to their teaching)—using information supplied by them we were enabled to go through it and find that most was of the Savior's true teaching, but that some things were added, which we list below for you.[62]

Unfortunately Eusebius did not reproduce the list.

The Churches of Asia Minor

16
PAPIAS OF HIERAPOLIS

Eusebius calls Papias "exceedingly limited mentally" (*Church History* 3.39.13) because he believed in the establishment of the Kingdom on earth for a thousand years, a doctrine derived from Jewish apocalyptic and in Eusebius's view outmoded. Apparently he was bishop in the early second century. His only known writing was the *Exegesis of the Dominical Oracles*.

Preface

1. I will not hesitate to set down in writing for you whatever I used to learn well from the elders and remembered well, maintaining the truth about them. For not like the many did I enjoy those who spoke the most but those who taught the truth, not those who delivered alien commands but those who delivered the commands given by the Lord to faith from the Truth itself [John 14:6]. But if by chance anyone came who had followed the elders, I inquired about the words of the elders: what Andrew or Peter said or Philip or Thomas or James or John or Matthew or any other of the Lord's disciples, or what Aristion and the elder John, the Lord's disciples, say. For I did not suppose that materials from books would help me as much as materials from a living and surviving voice.[63]

2. [from Book 1] The first Christians called those who practised purity before God by the name "children."[64]

3. [from Book 2] Papias of Hierapolis, an eyewitness of this, says in the second book of the *Dominical Oracles* that John was killed by Jews [cf. Mark 10:38–39].[65]

4. [from Book 4] There will be enjoyment of foods in the resurrection.[66]

5. The days will come when vines will grow up, each with 10,000 vines and in one vine 10,000 branches and in one branch 10,000 vine-shoots and in each vine-shoot 10,000 clusters and in each cluster 10,000 grapes; and each grape when pressed will give twenty-five measures of wine.[67] And when anyone takes one of those holy vine-shoots, another will shout, "I am a better vine-shoot; take me; bless the Lord through me." Likewise a grain of wheat will bring forth 10,000 ears and each ear will have 10,000 grains and each grain, five two-pound measures of first-grade fine flour; and the rest of the fruits and seeds and herbs in harmony follow them; and all the animals, using those foods which are received from the earth, become peaceful and in harmony with one another, being subject to men in complete submission. These things are credible to believers. And Judas the traitor, who did not believe, asked, "How then will such creatures be brought to perfection by the Lord?" The Lord said, "Those who come in them will see."[68]

6. Judas walked about in this world as a great example of impiety. His flesh was so bloated that he could not pass where a wagon could easily pass through, not even the mass of his head. For his eyelids were so swollen so that he could not see light. His eyes could not be made visible even by a surgeon's speculum (*dioptra*). Such was his decline in his external appearance. And his genitals were more shameful and enlarged beyond the parts of any other, and from his whole body there flowed pus and worms which tormented him when he relieved himself. After many torments and punishments he died on his own property [the "potter's field"]; and because of the stench the property remains deserted and uninhabited to this day. No one can go to that place to this day unless he holds his nose, so great was the discharge that took place through his flesh and on the ground.[69]

7. Papias mentions that he had a wonderful story from the daughters of Philip. For he relates that the resurrection of a dead body took place in his day; and he tells of another miraculous happening concerned with Justus surnamed Barsabbas [Acts 1:23]: that he drank a deadly poison and by the Lord's grace suffered no ill effects.

And the same writer has quoted other things also as coming to him from unwritten tradition; for instance, certain strange parables of the Savior and teachings of his, and some other things of a rather mythical character. Among them is his statement that after the resurrection of the dead there will be a period of a thousand years, when the kingdom of Christ will be set up in a material order on the earth.[70]

8. Those who are worthy of life will go there; others will enjoy the delights of paradise; others will possess the brightness of the city; for everywhere the

Lord will be seen as those who see him are worthy. There is this distinction among those who bring forth fruit a hundredfold and sixtyfold and thirty-fold [Matt. 13:23]: the first will be taken up into heaven, the second will live in paradise, and the third will inhabit the city. For this reason the Lord said, "In my Father's [house] are many mansions" [John 14:2]. For all things are God's, and he provides a suitable dwelling for everyone.[71]

9. He gave some of the angels charge over earthly affairs and commanded them to rule well; but their order ended in nothing.[72]

10. [Papias and others] understand the whole six-days' work [of the creation] in reference to Christ and the Church.[73]

The Gospels

11. This also the elder used to say: "Mark, having been the interpreter of Peter, wrote accurately though not in order all that he recalled of what was either said or done by the Lord. For he neither heard the Lord nor was he a follower of his, but at a later date, as I said, of Peter, who used to adapt his instructions to the needs [of his hearers], but not with a view to putting the Dominical oracles together in orderly fashion. So Mark did no wrong in thus writing some things as he recalled them. For he kept a single aim in view: not to omit anything of what he heard, nor to state anything falsely."[74]

12. Matthew then compiled the oracles in the Hebrew language, but everyone interpreted them as he was able.[75]

13. Beginning of the discussion of According to John. The Gospel of John was revealed and given to the churches by John, still alive in the body, as Papias the Hieropolitan, the beloved disciple of John, reported in the five exoteric[76] (that is, last) books. He transcribed the gospel as John correctly dictated it. But the heretic Marcion, when disapproved by him because his ideas were contrary, was removed by John. He [Marcion] had brought writings or epistles to him [John] from the brothers who were in Pontus.[77]

This is so thoroughly garbled that it is impossible to recover historical information from it.

17
CLAUDIUS APOLLINARIS OF HIERAPOLIS

Eusebius lists the works of Papias's later successor Apollinaris (around 175): an address to Marcus Aurelius and five books: *Against the Greeks*; *Concerning Truth*, volumes 1 and 2; *Against the Jews*, volumes

1 and 2; and the later treatise *Against the Heresy of the Phrygians.* Very few fragments from any of the works survive, however.[78]

To Marcus Aurelius (?)

1. From that time the legion which through prayer had performed this miracle received from the emperor a name suited to the deed, being called "thundering" in the Roman tongue.[79]

Apollinaris is the first Christian witness to the miracle, which Marcus Aurelius apparently depicted on his column, now in the Piazza Colonna at Rome. The question about the miracle was not whether it happened but why it happened, as Eusebius claims.[80] Four explanations were given:

(1) Zeus/Jupiter, depicted on the coins and perhaps on the column of Marcus Aurelius, answered a prayer by the emperor.[81]

(2) The senatorial historian Dio Cassius says that "there is a story that a certain Arnouphis, an Egyptian magician, had invoked various demons by spells (*manganeiai*), notably Hermes of the Air,"[82] and a similar account is found in the *Suda*.[83] Arnouphis himself appears in an inscription from Aquileia[84] which reads thus: "Arnouphis the Egyptian sacred scribe and Terentius Priscus, to the goddess present here"—no doubt Isis.[85] "Hermes of the Air" may be the Egyptian god Thoth-Shou.[86]

(3) The theurgist Julian, son of another religious writer in the time of Marcus, was also said to have worked the miracle.[87]

(4) Christians soon held that their god had responded to prayers by a legion later described as entirely Christian.[88]

In the eleventh century the patriarch Xiphilinus criticized the story about Arnouphis, arguing that "Marcus is not reported to have taken pleasure in the company of magicians (*magoi*) or in witchcraft (*goéteiai*)."[89] Presumably Xiphilinus's point is based on Marcus's *Meditations* 1.6, which states that from his tutor Diognetus Marcus had learned "to disbelieve the claims of sorcerers (*terateuomenoi*) and magicians (*goétoi*) about incantations (*epôdoi*) and exorcism of spirits and the like."[90]

Such a story is not unique, in any event. Dio Cassius tells how a century earlier the Roman general Hosidius Geta ran out of water while pursuing a Moorish force into the African desert. Fortunately an allied native "persuaded him to try some incantations (*epôdai*) and enchantments (*manganeiai*), telling him that as a result of such rites abundant water had often been given to his people." Immediately there was such a downpour that the Romans' thirst was abolished and the barbarians, alarmed because the divine power seemed to be aiding the Romans, ended their resistance.[91]

2. [*On the Pascha*] There are some who through ignorance are contentious about these matters, suffering for a pardonable offence; for ignorance does not receive accusation but needs instruction. And they say that on the 14th day the Lord ate the lamb with his disciples, but on the great day of unleavened bread he suffered, and they describe Matthew as speaking [Matt. 26:17] as they have understood—wherefore their understanding is not in agreement with the Law, and according to them the Gospels seem to disagree.[92]

3. The 14th is the true Passover of the Lord, the great sacrifice, the Son of God in place of the lamb, the bound one who bound the strong, the judged one who is judge of living and dead, and the one given over to the hands of sinners to be crucified who is the one exalted on the wings of the unicorn, who poured out from his side the two purifiers water and blood; and the one who was buried on the day of the Passover, with a stone placed on the tomb [is]. . . .[93]

4. [*Against the Heresy of the Phrygians*] But that you may also know this, that the work of this lying party of the so-called New Prophecy is abominated by the whole brotherhood in the world, I [Serapion of Antioch, Section 15] have sent you also a letter of Claudius Apollinaris, who was the most blessed bishop in Hierapolis in Asia. In this epistle the signatures of various bishops are extant, one of whom signed thus: "I Aurelius Quirinus, a martyr, pray that you may be well." Another, in this fashion: "Aelius Publius Julius, bishop from Debeltum, the colony in Thrace. As God in heaven lives, I swear that the blessed Sotas of Anchialus wanted to cast out Priscilla's demon, and the hypocrites would not let him." And the autograph signatures of a large number of other bishops who agreed with them are extant in the said letter.[94]

18
MELITO OF SARDIS

Melito of Sardis was a contemporary of Apollinaris of Hierapolis. Tertullian, writing as a Montanist in his lost treatise *On Ecstasy*, spoke of

Melito's *elegans et declamatorium ingenium* and said that many Catholics thought he was a prophet.[95] Critical or laudatory? I have omitted Melito's lengthy paschal homily, since it is not a fragment, and generally follow S. G. Hall's judgments on the fragments as well as his numbering.[96]

1. [*To Antoninus*] What never happened before, the race of the godly is persecuted, harassed by new decrees throughout Asia. For shameless informers and lovers of other people's goods, take advantage of the decrees and openly plunder us, night and day robbing innocent persons. If this is done by your order, let it be done properly. For a just king would never consider acting unjustly, and we gladly accept the prize of such a death. We make only this petition to you, that you yourself will first take note of those who cause such strife and justly judge whether they deserve death and punishment or safety and security.

But if this decision and this new ordinance, not suitable even against hostile barbarians, are not from you, all the more we beg you not to leave us suffering such a public persecution.

Our philosophy first flourished among barbarians, but after flowering among your peoples during the powerful reign of your ancestor Augustus it became a blessing especially for your empire. For from that time the might of the Romans grew to be something great and splendid. You, the object of men's hopes, have succeeded to it and will continue, along with your son [Commodus] if you protect the philosophy which was cradled and took its beginning with Augustus, and which your ancestors honored along with the other cults. This is the greatest proof that our teaching flourished for the good along with the empire as it happily started out, that from the reign of Augustus no evil has befallen it but, on the contrary, everything has been splendid and praiseworthy in accordance with the prayers of all. Alone among all, persuaded by certain malignant persons, Nero and Domitian wanted to bring our teaching into ill repute; and from these persons false charges have continued to flow against such people by irrational custom. But your pious fathers corrected their ignorance, many times rebuking the many who dared to arouse disturbances against these men. Among them was your grandfather Hadrian, who clearly wrote to the proconsul Fundanus, governor of Asia, and your father, when you were administering everything with him, wrote to the cities, notably to the Larissans and the Thessalonians and the Athenians and all the Greeks. And in your case, since you hold the same opinion of these men that they did and have far more love of humanity and philosophical concern, we are even more persuaded that you will do everything that we ask of you.[97]

2. [After many things also handed down by Justin] We are not worshipers of stones without sense-perception, but we worship the only God, who is before all and over all, and his Christ, who is the Logos of God before all ages.[98]

Old Testament Canon

3. [*Selections*] Melito to his brother Onesimus, greeting. Since in your zeal for the word you often asked to have selections from the Law and the Prophets about the Savior and our faith as a whole, and moreover you wanted to learn the exact truth about the ancient books, their number and their order, I was zealous to perform such a task, knowing your zeal for the faith and love for the study of the word, and aware that in your yearning for God you esteem these things above everything else as you contend for the prize of eternal salvation. Therefore, having visited the East and come to the place where these matters were proclaimed and done, and having learned exactly which the books of the Old Covenant are, I am sending you the list of them which is given below. These are their names: Of Moses, five books: Genesis, Exodus, Numbers, Leviticus, Deuteronomy; Jesus Nave [= Joshua], Judges, Ruth; four of Kingdoms; two of [Chronicles]; Psalms of David; of Solomon, Proverbs (also called Wisdom), Ecclesiastes, Song of Songs; Job; of the prophets, Isaiah, Jeremiah, the Twelve in a single book; Daniel; Ezekiel; Esdras. From these I have made the selections, dividing them into six books.[99]

4. [*On the Passover*] In the time of Servillius Paulus,[100] proconsul of Asia, at the time when Sagaris was martyred, there was much dispute in Laodicea about the Passover, which in those days fell at the time [when he was martyred], and these things were written.

Clement of Alexandria mentions this work in his own work *On the Passover*, which he says he composed because of Melito's writing.[101] The style of our fragment is so different from the *Paschal Homily* of Melito that it must come from another work (not a homily).

5. Absalom [title of Psalm 3] represents the Devil, who rose up against the kingdom of Christ.

Having simply mentioned this, Melito does not add any detail on the passage.[102]

[Fragment 6 is probably not genuine, and Fragment 7 is from the *Paschal Homily*.]

8. [*On Baptism*[103]] What sort of gold or silver or bronze or iron is not made red hot and dipped in water, in one case to be brightened by the color, in another to be tempered by the dipping? The whole earth, too, is washed by rains and rivers, and when washed yields well. Likewise the land of Egypt when washed by a swollen river increases its output, fills out its sheaf, and yields a hundredfold through the good washing. Even the air is washed by the downpour of the showers. The many-colored rainbow, mother of rains, is washed when she swells rivers down channels, summoned by a wind that brings water.

If you wish to see the heavenly bodies baptized, turn now to the ocean, and there I will show you a novel sight: the sea outspread and without limits, the unplumbable deep, the immeasurable ocean, pure water, the baptistery of the sun and the lampstand of the stars and the bath of the moon.

Learn from me reliably how they are mystically washed. The sun, opening the course of the day with fiery horses, by the movement of the course becomes fiery and shines like a torch. It burns up the middle zone of its course; when one sees it nearby it is as if it struck the earth with ten brilliant lightnings. Then it is constrained to go down into the ocean. Like a bronze ball, filled with fire inside, radiant with light, it makes a loud sound and shines with light as it is washed in the cold water; but its inner fire is not put out but shines, burning again. So it is with the sun. On fire like lightning, it is washed in cold water but not put out, for it has an unsleeping fire. Washed in a mystic baptism, it greatly rejoices, having the water for nourishment. Though one and the same, the sun rises as new for men; intensified by the abyss, cleansed by the washing. It has driven away the night-time darkness and generated the luminous day. On the same course the movements of the stars and the moon are accomplished by nature. They are washed in the baptistery of the sun, as good disciples. The stars with the moon follow the track of the sun, for they have a pure light.

Now if the sun with the stars and the moon is washed in the ocean, why would not the Christ too be washed in the Jordan? King of the heavens and ruler of the creation, sun of the east, who appeared both to the dead in Hades and to mortals in the world—the only Sun who rose from the sky![104]

9. He was bound as a ram and shorn as a lamb and as a sheep he was led to slaughter and crucified as a lamb; he carried the wood on his shoulders as he was led up to be slain like Isaac by his Father.

But Christ suffered while Isaac did not suffer, for he was a model (*typos*) for the Christ who was to suffer. But by becoming the model of Christ he caused astonishment and fear for men. For it was a new mystery to behold, a son led by his father to a mountain for slaughter, whose feet he bound, whom he put on the wood of the offering, preparing with zeal the things for his slaughter. But Isaac was silent, bound like a ram, not opening his mouth or uttering a sound. Not frightened by the sword nor alarmed at the fire nor grieved by the suffering, he bore the model of the Lord with endurance. Thus Isaac was offered in the midst with feet bound like a ram, and Abraham stood by and held the naked sword, not ashamed to kill his son.[105]

10. A ram appeared for slaughter on behalf of Isaac the righteous one so that Isaac might be loosed from bonds. That ram when slain redeemed Isaac; thus also the Lord when slain saved us and when bound freed us and when sacrificed redeemed us.

11. The Lord was a lamb like the ram which Abraham saw caught in a Sabek-bush; but the bush displayed the cross and that place, Jerusalem, and the lamb, the Lord in fetters for slaughter.

[I omit Hall's Fragments 12–16 and New Fragments 2–3 as either suspect or unusually repetitive.]

17. [Hymn] Praise the Father with a hymn, you saints!
Sing to the Mother, you virgins!
We praise, we highly exalt, saints.
You have been exalted, brides and bridegrooms,
For you have found your bridgroom, Christ.
Drink of the wine, brides and bridegrooms.

This fragment appears just after Melito's *Paschal Homily* in Papyrus Bodmer XIII. Perler comments, "This hymn could be part of the Quartodeciman Paschal liturgy. It would have been sung after baptism and before the agape-eucharist."[106] But it may well not come from Melito.

19
PRESBYTERS OF ASIA

1. Though the jewel emerald is greatly prized by some, yet glass when skillfully made like it puts it to shame, as long as no one is present who can test it and prove it was made artificially. And when copper is mixed with silver, who can easily test if it is pure?[107]

2. Venturesome and bold is the soul heated by empty air.[108]

3. Idol-maker Marcus, inspector of portents,
Expert in astrology and the magic art,
Through which you confirm your false teachings,
Showing signs to those whom you deceive,
The works of apostate power,
Which your father Satan always provides for you
To work by the power of the angel Azazel;
He has you as a forerunner of godless wickedness.[109]

4. Gypsum mixes badly with the milk of God.[110]

5. God transferred the curse [upon Adam] to the earth, lest it continue against man.[111]

6. The measureless Father is himself measured in the Son; the Son is the measure of the Father, for he contains him.[112]

7.a. The correction provided by the scriptures was enough for the ancients in those matters which they performed without the counsel of the Spirit. b. The scripture accused Solomon sufficiently so that all flesh should not glory in the Lord's sight.[113] c. Therefore we should not be proud, nor upbraid the ancients, but rather ourselves fear lest after the recognition of Christ we should do something displeasing to God and, no longer having remission of sins, be excluded from his kingdom.[114] d. By ignoring the vindications of God and his plans, opponents of the Old Testament condemn themselves.[115] e. In regard to the sins for which the scriptures themselves blame the patriarchs and prophets, we should not reprove them or become like Ham, who laughed at his father's shame and fell into wickedness; but rather give thanks to God for them, since at the coming of our Lord their sins were remitted; for he said they gave thanks and rejoiced in our salvation [John 8:56].[116] We should not accuse those whom the scriptures do not blame, but who are simply described, for we are not more diligent than God and we cannot be above our master, but we ought to seek for the "type." For nothing is without meaning in those things that are described in the scriptures even without moralizing.[117]

8. The Son is understood in two ways, one according to the nature by which he was born a son; the other according to what he was made, for there is a difference between "born" and "made."[118]

9. Those who were transported were transported into Paradise, for Paradise was prepared for righteous and inspired men. When the apostle was transported to it he heard words which cannot be spoken [2 Cor. 12:4] to us now; and there the transported ones remain until the end, prepared in advance for incorruption.[119]

10. Through the divine stretching forth of his hands he led the two peoples to one God. For there are two hands because the two peoples are

dispersed to the ends of the earth, but one head, for God is one, who is over all and through all and in us all [Eph. 4:6].[120]

11. All the genuine and ancient copies of the Apocalypse, as well as those who saw John and taught us, agree that the number of the beast [Rev. 13:18] is 666. Some have made a mistake and given a number that is 50 short; instead of six decades they want it to be one[121] (616 for 666).

20
POLYCRATES OF EPHESUS

For us, then, we keep the day [14th Nisan] without tampering with it, neither adding nor subtracting. For indeed in Asia great luminaries have fallen asleep, who will rise again on the day of the Lord's appearing, when he comes with glory from heaven to seek out all his saints: Philip, one of the twelve apostles, who has fallen asleep in Hierapolis, [as have] also his two daughters who grew old in virginity and his other daughter, who lived in the Holy Spirit and rests at Ephesus; and moreover John too, he who leaned back on the Lord's breast [John 13:25] and was a priest, wearing the sacerdotal plate, both martyr and teacher. He has fallen asleep at Ephesus. Moreover Polycarp too, at Smyrna both bishop and martyr; and Thraseas, both bishop and martyr, of Eumeneia, who has fallen asleep at Smyrna. And why need I mention Sagaris, bishop and martyr, who has fallen asleep at Laodicea?[122] or the blessed Papirius, or Melito the eunuch who in all things lived in the Holy Spirit, who lies at Sardis awaiting the visitation from heaven, when he shall rise from the dead? These all observed the 14th day for the Pascha (Passover) according to the Gospel, in no way deviating therefrom but following the rule of faith.

And moreover I also, Polycrates, least among all of you, [observe it] according to the tradition of my relatives, some of whom also I have followed closely. Seven of my relatives were bishops, and I am the eighth. And my relatives always observed the day when the people put away the leaven.[123] Therefore I for my part, brothers, who count 65 years in the Lord and have conversed with the brothers from all parts of the world and have traversed the entire range of holy Scripture, am not frightened by threats. For those better than me have said, "We must obey God rather than men" [Peter in Acts 5:29].

But I could mention the bishops present with me, whom I summoned when you yourselves wanted me to summon them. And were I to write their names, their number would be great. But they, who know my littleness, approved my letter, knowing that I did not wear my grey hairs in vain but that I have ever lived in Christ Jesus.[124]

21
ABERCIUS OF HIEROPOLIS

There was a small city in Phrygia named Hieropolis (as distinct from Hierapolis), and this is where the epitaph of Aberkios, now in the Vatican, comes from. It is unclear whether or not this Aberkios is to be identified with the Avircius Marcellus mentioned by Eusebius.[125]

> I a citizen of the elect city erected this
> in my lifetime, that I might have before me a place for my body;
> my name is Aberkios, a disciple of the pure Shepherd
> who feeds the flocks of sheep on mountains and plains,
> who has great all-seeing eyes;
> he taught me . . . faithful scriptures.
> To Rome he sent me to see my king
> and to see the queen, gold-robed and gold-sandaled;
> a people I saw there which has a splendid seal.
> And I saw the plain and all the towns of Syria, and Nisibis,
> crossing the Euphrates; but everywhere I met fellows;
> Paul was my companion, and Faith everywhere led the way
> and served food everywhere, the Fish from the spring
> —immense, pure, which the pure Virgin caught
> and gave to her friends to eat forever,
> with good wine, giving the cup with the loaf.
>
> These things I Aberkios said to be written thus in my presence.
> I am truly seventy-two years old.
> No one is to put anyone else into my tomb; otherwise he
> is to pay the Roman treasury 2000 gold pieces, and my
> good native city of Hieropolis 1000 gold pieces.[126]

22
APOLLONIUS OF EPHESUS

Apollonius was evidently well acquainted with Montanism as well as the charges against it. His attack suggests that the Montanist leaders were more avaricious than spiritually innovative. Montanists took the attack so seriously that Tertullian wrote Book 7 of his (lost) treatise *On Ecstasy* against Apollonius, according to Jerome.[127] The fragments deal primarily with Montanist prophets and prophecy.

1. But his works and teaching show what kind of new-fangled teacher [Montanus] is. This is he who taught dissolutions of marriages, who laid down laws on fasting, who gave the name Jerusalem to Pepuza and Tymion in his desire to draw people from everywhere,[128] who appointed agents for collecting money, who has devised his scheme for receiving gifts under the name of "offerings," who has supplied salaries to those who preach his doctrine so that the teaching of it may be more effective by means of gluttony.

We show, therefore, that these prophetesses were the very first to leave their husbands from the time when they were filled by the spirit. How then did they tell lies, calling Priscilla a virgin?

Does not every scripture [*Didache* 11–12] seem to you to forbid a prophet to receive gifts and money? Therefore, when I see the prophetess possessed of gold and silver and costly apparel, how can I fail to reject her?

Moreover, Themiso too, he who is clothed with plausible covetousness, who did not bear the sign of confession but put off his chains thanks to a large sum of money and (though this fact should have made him humble) boasts himself a martyr—this man, imitating the Apostle, dared to compose a "catholic epistle" and in it to instruct those whose faith had surpassed his to contend with empty-sounding words and to utter blasphemy against the Lord, the apostles, and the holy Church.

But not to speak of many, let the prophetess tell us about Alexander, who calls himself a martyr, with whom she banquets, to whom many do reverence. It is not for us to speak of his robberies and the other deeds of daring for which he has been punished—the record office preserves the tale of them. Which, then, of the two forgives the other's sins? Does the prophet forgive the martyr his robberies, or the martyr forgive the prophet his deeds of covetousness? For though the Lord has said, "Get no gold or silver or two coats" [Matt. 10:9–10], they have transgressed in absolute contradiction by getting these forbidden things. For we shall show that those whom they call prophets and martyrs get their petty gains not only from the rich but also from the poor and orphans and widows. And if they are confident, let them take their stand on this and come to a definite agreement on this understanding, that if convicted they may cease to transgress, at least for the future. For one ought to prove the fruits of the prophet: for the tree is known by its fruit. But that those who wish may know about

Alexander, he has been convicted by Aemilius Frontinus,[129] proconsul at Ephesus, not because of the Name but because of the robberies he committed, being already an apostate. Then, by falsely claiming the name of the Lord, he was released after deceiving the Christians there, and his own community from which he came would not receive him because he was a robber. Those who wish to learn about him have the public archives of Asia. And yet the prophet knows nothing about the one with whom he associated for many years! In exposing this man we also expose through him his claim to be a prophet. We can show the same in the case of many; and if they have the courage, let them stand the exposure.

If they deny that their prophets have received gifts, let them agree on this point, that if they are convicted of having received them they are not prophets; and we will supply countless demonstrations of the fact. But one must prove all the fruits of a prophet. Tell me, does a prophet dye his hair? Does a prophet paint his eyelids? Does a prophet love adornment? Does a prophet play at gaming tables and dice? Does a prophet lend money at interest? Let them agree as to whether these things are permitted or not, and for my part I will show that they took place among them.[130]

23
ANONYMOUS AGAINST MONTANISM

It is a long and very considerable time, beloved Avircius Marcellus, since you urged me to write some kind of treatise against the heresy of the followers of Miltiades, as they are called. Yet I have somehow held back until now, not through lack of ability to refute falsehood and bear witness to the truth, but from fear and extreme caution lest by chance I might seem to some to be adding a new article or clause to the word of the New Covenant of the gospel, to which no one who has proposed to live according to the gospel itself may add and from which no one may take away.

Conference at Ancyra

But when recently I came to Ancyra in Galatia and found the local church ringing with the noise of this new (not as they say, prophecy, but much rather, as will be shown) false prophecy, with the Lord's help we discoursed to the best of our ability in the church for many days on every one of these same points, as well as on those which they proposed. The result was that the church rejoiced greatly and was confirmed in the truth, while those on the contrary side were crushed for the moment and the opposition was put to grief. So when the local presbyters asked us to leave behind some memorandum of what had been said against those who oppose the word of truth when our fellow-presbyter Zoticus of Otrous was also present, though we did not do this, we promised to write it here, should the Lord permit, and send it to them speedily.

The Origins of Montanism

Their opposition, then, and their recent schismatical heresy as regards the Church, arose in this way. There is reported to be a village in Mysia bordering on Phrygia, by the name of Ardabau. It is said that there a recent convert to the faith named Montanus—while Gratus was proconsul of Asia[131]—in the immeasurable longing of his soul for preeminence first gave the Adversary a passage into his heart; and that moved by the spirit he suddenly fell into a state of possession, as it were, and abnormal ecstasy, to such an extent that he became frenzied and began to babble and utter strange sounds, that is to say, prophesying in a manner contrary to what the Church had received by tradition from generation to generation from the beginning. Some of those who heard his spurious utterances at that time were annoyed at him as at one possessed and tormented by a demon, the prey of a spirit of error and a disturber of the people. So they rebuked him and strove to check his speaking, mindful of the injunction and warning of the Lord to guard watchfully against the coming of false prophets [Matt. 7:15]. But others were puffed up as if at a prophetical gift of the Holy Spirit and filled with no slight conceit and forgetful of the Lord's injunction. They therefore called forth this maddening and cajoling spirit which was deceiving the people, by which they were beguiled and deceived, so that it could no longer be checked and silenced. And by some art, or rather by the use of such an evil artifice, the Devil secretly stirred up and inflamed the minds which had lost the true faith in sleep, those of the disobedient persons whose ruin he had devised and by whom, accordingly, he was honored. He raised up two women as well and so filled them with the spurious spirit that they too babbled in a frenzied, inopportune and unnatural manner, like the aforementioned man [Montanus]. And the spirit pronounced blessed those who rejoiced and took pride in him and puffed them up with the greatness of his promises; at times, however, he would administer shrewd and plausible rebukes to their face so that he might seem capable of reproving also. Nevertheless, few were thus deceived by the Phrygians.

Montanism Rejected by Asian Synods

This arrogant spirit taught them to blaspheme the whole universal Church under heaven because the spirit of false prophecy received neither honor nor admission into it. For when the faithful throughout Asia had met frequently and at many places in Asia for this purpose, and on examination of the new-fangled teachings had pronounced them profane and rejected the heresy, these persons were expelled from the Church and shut off from its fellowship.

Montanist Prophecy

Book 2. Since, then, they used to call us slayers of the prophets [Matt. 23:31] because we did not accept their prophets of unbridled tongue (these, they say, are the ones whom the Lord promised to send to the people), let them answer us before God: Is there a single one, good people, of those who began their talk with Montanus and the women, who was persecuted by Jews or killed by lawless men? None. Or were any of them seized and crucified for the Name's sake? No. Or, for that matter, were any of the women ever scourged or stoned in the synagogues of the Jews? Never anywhere. Montanus and Maximilla are said to have died a different death; for it is said that each of them was inspired by a maddening spirit to kill themselves, though not together, and widespread rumor at the time of their death held that they died like the traitor Judas. It is also said that the remarkable man Theodotus, so to speak the first steward of their so-called prophecy, was sometimes taken up and, when he fell into ecstasy and entrusted himself to the spirit of deceit, was raised to the heavens but was whirled to the ground and so met a wretched end. In any event they say it happened thus. But without seeing, my friend, let us not suppose that we know any such things, for perhaps Montanus and Theodotus and the aforementioned woman died thus; perhaps not.

And let not the spirit which spoke in the person of Maximilla say, in the same book *According to Asterius Urbanus*, "I am driven as a wolf from the sheep. I am not a wolf. I am word and spirit and power." But let him show clearly the power that is in the spirit, let him bring convincing proof of it, and by the spirit let him force an acknowledgement from those who were then present to prove and discourse with the talkative spirit. Approved men and bishops, Zoticus from the village of Cumana and Julian from Apamea, whose mouths the followers of Priscilla muzzled, not letting them refute the false spirit which was deceiving the people.

Is it not evident that this too is false? For it is more than thirteen years today since the woman died, and in the world there has been neither local nor universal war but, by God's mercy, continuing peace even for Christians.

Montanist Martyrs

Book 3. So when they have been refuted in all their arguments and have no reply to make, they try to take refuge in martyrs, saying that they have many martyrs and that this is a reliable proof of the power of the alleged prophetic spirit among them. But this, as it appears, is absolutely untrue. Some other heresies have immense numbers of martyrs, but surely we shall not give them our assent because of this or acknowledge that they possess the truth. To take them first, those called Marcionites from the heresy of Marcion say that they have immense numbers of martyrs of Christ, but as regards Christ himself they do not truly acknowledge him.

It is doubtless for this reason that whenever those called from the Church to martyrdom for the true faith encounter any of the so-called martyrs from the heresy of the Phrygians they separate from them and are perfected without having fellowship with them, for they do not wish to assent to the spirit which spoke through Montanus and the women. And it is an evident fact that this is true, and that it took place in our time at Apamea on the Meander among those martyrs of Eumeneia who were the companions of Gaius and Alexander.

Montanist Prophecy

I found these things in a certain treatise of theirs in which they attack that treatise of our brother Alcibiades [Miltiades] in which he shows that a prophet ought not to speak in a state of ecstasy; and I abridged them . . . but the false prophet [speaks] in ecstasy, and boldness and fearlessness follow him. He begins with voluntary ignorance but turns to involuntary madness of soul, as said before. But they cannot show that any prophet either in the Old Testament or in the New was inspired in this way. They cannot boast of Agabus [Acts 11:28], Judas, Silas [Acts 15:32], the daughters of Philip [Acts 21:9], Ammia in Philadelphia, Quadratus, or any others who do not belong to them. . . . For if the Montanist women were successors of Quadratus and Ammia in Philadelphia in the prophetic gift, as they say, let them show who among them were successors to the followers of Montanus and the women, for the Apostle lays it down [perhaps 1 Cor. 1:7] that the prophetic gift will be in the whole Church until the final coming; but this they could not show, since it is already the 14th year from the death of Maximilla.[132]

24
MONTANIST ORACLES

Here we follow the order provided by R. E. Heine for the authentic oracles,[133] omitting those he considers questionable.

Oracles of Montanus

1. "I am the Lord God Almighty dwelling in man."[134]

2. "I am neither an angel nor an envoy, but I the Lord God, the Father, have come."[135]

3. "Behold, man is as a lyre, and I hover over him as a plectrum; man sleeps but I watch; behold, the Lord is removing the hearts of men and giving them [new] hearts."[136]

4. "Why do you say 'the superman who is saved'? Because the righteous will shine a hundred times brighter than the sun, and even the little ones among you who are saved, a hundred times brighter than the moon."[137]

Oracles of Maximilla

5. "I am driven from the sheep as a wolf. I am not a wolf. I am word, spirit, and power."[138]

6. "After me there will no longer be a prophet, but the End."[139]

7. "Do not listen to me, but listen to Christ."[140]

8. "The Lord sent me as a partisan of this labor, a revealer of this covenant, an interpreter of this promise, forced, whether I will or not, to learn the knowledge of God."[141]

Oracles of Prisca (Priscilla)

9. "They are flesh, yet they hate the flesh."[142]

10. "For continence brings harmony, and they see visions and, bowing their heads, they also hear distinct voices, saving and mysterious."[143]

Oracles of Priscilla or Quintilla

11. "Appearing as a woman clothed in a shining robe, Christ came to me [in sleep]; he put wisdom into me and revealed to me that this place is sacred and that here Jerusalem will come down from heaven [cf. Rev. 21:2]."[144]

"Here" means an area between the small villages of Pepouza and Timion in Asia Minor, venerated by Montanists (see chap. 23). See W. Tabbernee, "Portals of the Montanist New Jerusalem: The Discovery of Pepouza and Tymion," *Journal of Early Christian Studies* 11 (2003), 87–93.

Unassigned Oracles

12. "The Church is able to forgive a sin, but I will not use it lest they commit other crimes."[145]

13. "You are exposed to public reproach? It is for your good. He who is not reproached by men is reproached by God. Do not be disconcerted; your righteousness has brought you into the midst [of all]. Why are you disconcerted, since you are gaining praise? Your power arises when you are seen by men."[146]

14. "Do not hope to die in bed or in abortion or in languishing fevers, but in martyrdom, so that he who suffered for you may be glorified."[147]

The Churches of Greece

25
QUADRATUS OF ATHENS

Eusebius says that Quadratus delivered an apology to Hadrian, presumably when the emperor visited Athens in 125 or 129. The one fragment contrasts the permanent deeds of "our Savior" with the impermanent deeds perhaps of someone else's savior (Hadrian himself was often called *sôtér*).[148]

But our Savior's works were permanent, for they were real. Those who had been cured or rose from the dead did not just appear to be cured or risen but were ever present, not only during the Savior's stay on earth but also after his departure. They remained for a considerable period, so that some of them even reached our times.[149]

26
DIONYSIUS OF CORINTH

In the *Church History* (4.23) Eusebius relies on a dossier of letters from Dionysius, bishop of Corinth, to churches "in foreign lands" and to some individuals, in the time when Soter was bishop of Rome (166–175). Eusebius gives brief descriptions of the letters and quotes from a few of them.[150] He begins with letters to two churches in Greece, teaching "orthodoxy" to the Lacedaemonians (Lacedaemon [Sparta] was a *civitas libera* under the Romans) and commending peace and unity, and calling on the Athenians for faith and a "polity" in accord with the gospel while rebuking them for their virtual apostasy after the martyrdom of their bishop Publius. He praises Quadratus for zealously reuniting them and mentions that Dionysius the Areopagite (Acts 17:34) had been their first bishop. Turning to the Christians of Nicomedia (the capital of Bithynia), he attacks the heresy of Marcion, who originally came from nearby Pontus. When he praises the church of Gortyna in southern Crete (the capital city of Crete), the other Cretan churches, and Philip (of Gortyna) for their attested good deeds (a conventional form of address?), he warns them, too, against heresy. In addition, he writes to Amastris and the other churches of Pontus, says that Bacchylides and Elpistus had asked him to write, and names their bishop Palmas. Exhorting them on marriage and chastity, he "commands" them to take back those suspected of falling away into misconduct or heresy.

There is also a letter to Pinytos bishop of Cnossus in northern Crete (whose city, like Corinth, was a Roman colony), urging him "not to lay a heavy compulsory burden of chastity on the brothers but to consider the weakness of the many." Pinytos, in turn, urged Dionysius to nourish his people with more solid food, not just milk, lest they "be caught unaware by old age while still treated as children" (cf. 1 Cor. 3:1–2; also "like children," 14:20).

An important letter is addressed to Soter of Rome, praising the church's contributions to "many churches" for the (Christian) poor and mine workers. He notes that a letter from Soter (perhaps sending funds) is sometimes read in the Corinthian church, as is the letter sent through Clement. After noting (in another letter?) that heretics have falsified his letters, Dionysius finally "imparts the proper spiritual food" to a woman named Chrysophora.

Pierre Nautin has provided a rational analysis of this little collection of Dionysius's letters.[151] The correspondence must have begun after Dionysius wrote to the church at Amastris in Pontus to oppose the rigorism of its bishop, Palmas, and advocate the readmission of penitents after any kind of sin. Palmas then denounced Dionysius to Soter, bishop of Rome, and Soter wrote Dionysius, giving him at least partial support. Dionysius claimed that his own words had been misquoted and stressed his own loyalty. The bishops of Gortyna and Cnossus in Crete were engaged in a similar conflict when Dionysius supported Philip of Gortyna against Pinytus of Cnossus and his view of continence as obligatory. In addition, Dionysius tried to end a schism at Lacedaemon and gave support to a new bishop in Athens by recalling the past history of the church there.

To Nautin's literary analysis we add a few notes on the historical situation in Corinth and in Pontus, especially at Amastris. The position of the Corinthian church was much the same as that of Corinth itself,[152] lying on trade routes to Italy and Asia Minor, to Crete and the Black Sea, and as the capital city of Achaea, ranking above Athens. Similarly Gortyna was the capital city of Crete, as Nicomedia was of Bithynia.

An inscription from Amastris in Pontus refers to "Tiberius Claudius Lepidus (son of Lepidus), high priest of [Augustus in] Pontus, prominent citizen."[153] Other references show that Lepidus's criticism of religious fakes was influential. Cagnat adduced a text from the satirist Lucian (see Fragment 1, page 9), who described the charlatan Alexander as claiming that "Pontus was full of atheists and Christians," and he "hated Amastris most of all the cities in Pontus because he knew that the followers of Lepidus and others like them were numerous in the city; and he would never deliver an oracle to an Amastrian."[154] Such was the situation around the time when Dionysius was writing to the Christians of Nicomedia and Amastris.[155] Later on, to be sure, Christian writers would claim that in the third century when Gregory Thaumaturgus became bishop of Neocaesarea in central Pontus only seventeen Christians lived there.[156] But, in fact, Christianity had a long history in the area. The first Christians to receive the canonical First Epistle of Peter are called "the elect sojourners of the dispersion in Pontus." The Roman legate Pliny (see chap. 2) reports that he has interrogated ex-Christians, apparently in Pontus, who claimed they had abandoned their religion as early as A.D. 90.[157] Considering this history, Dionysius had to reply to his critics in Pontus, especially when they asked him to take a more rigorous stand against backsliding. He had to maintain his position as the guardian of Greek cities to the north and east of Corinth.

1. *To the Romans.* For this has been your custom from the beginning: to do good in various ways to all the brothers, and to send supplies to many churches in every city, now relieving the poverty of the needy, now making provision for the brothers in the mines by the supplies you have customarily sent from the beginning. And thus as Romans you observe the hereditary custom of Romans, which your blessed bishop Soter has not only maintained but even advanced by abundantly providing the aid distributed for the use of the saints and by exhorting with blessed words the brothers who come up [to Rome], as a loving father exhorts his children.[158]

2. In these ways you also, by such an admonition, have united the planting that came from Peter and Paul of both the Romans and the Corinthians. For indeed both planted also in our Corinth, and likewise taught us; and likewise they also taught together in Italy and were martyred on the same occasion.[159]

3. This day, therefore, we spent as a holy Lord's day, in which we read your epistle, from the reading of which we shall always be able to obtain admonition, as also from the former epistle written to us through Clement.[160]

4. For when the brothers wanted me to write epistles I did so. And the apostles of the Devil have filled these with tares, cutting out some things and adding others;[161] for them the Woe is reserved. It is no wonder, therefore, if some have set themselves to tamper with the Dominical Scriptures as well, since they have also laid their designs against writing not classified among them.[162]

Besides these another epistle of Dionysius is extant, which he wrote to a Christian sister, Chrysophora. He writes what is suitable and imparts spiritual food to her.[163]

The Church of Carthage

27
ACTS OF THE SCILLITAN MARTYRS

The oldest document from the churches of [North] Africa is the Acts of the Scillitan Martyrs, apparently based on the court record of a hearing at Carthage on July 17, 180. The text is printed in G. Krüger, R. Knopf, and G. Ruhbach, *Ausgewählte Märtyrerakten* ([Tübingen: Mohr, 1965], 28–29) and H. Musurillo, *The Acts of the Christian Martyrs* ([Oxford: Clarendon, 1972], xxii–xxiii, 86–89).

The Interrogation

In the consulship of Praesens for the second time and Claudianus, on the sixteenth day before the Kalends of August, into the Senate House of Carthage were brought Speratus, Nartzalus and Cittinus, [Veturius, Felix, Aquilinus, Laetantius, Januaria, Generosa,] Donata, Secunda, Vestia,[164] to whom the proconsul Saturninus said, "You may receive pardon from our lord the emperor if you return to good sense." Speratus said, "We have never done evil, we have committed no iniquitous deed, we have never cursed; but when we were received badly we gave thanks; for we respect our ruler." The proconsul Saturninus said, "We too are religious, and our religion is simple: We swear by the Genius of our lord the emperor, and we pray for his safety, as you also should." Speratus said, "If you will calmly lend an ear, I will tell you the mystery of simplicity." Saturninus said, "I will not lend an ear to you who are about to say evil things about our rites; on the contrary, swear by the Genius of our lord the emperor." Speratus said, "I do not recognize the authority of this age; instead, I serve that God whom no man sees or can see with these eyes. I have not committed theft, but if I have bought anything I have paid the tax. For I recognize my Lord, the emperor of kings and of all nations."

Abandon Christianity

The proconsul Saturninus said to the rest, "Abandon this persuasion." Speratus said, "It is an evil persuasion to commit murder, to bear false witness." The proconsul Saturninus said, "Do not share in this madness." Cittinus said, "There is no one we fear except the Lord our God who is in heaven." Donata said, "Honor to Caesar as Caesar, but fear to God" [cf. 1 Pet. 2:17]. Vestia said, "I am a Christian." Secunda said, "What I am, I want to remain." The proconsul Saturninus said, "Do you persevere in being a Christian?" Speratus said, "I am a Christian," and they all agreed with him.

Postponement?

The proconsul Saturninus said, "Do you want some time to consider?" Speratus said, "In so just an affair there is no need to consider." The proconsul Saturninus said, "What things do you have in your box?" Speratus said, "The books, and the epistles of Paul, a just man." The proconsul Saturninus said, "Take a stay of thirty days and reconsider." Speratus again said, "I am a Christian"; and they all agreed with him.

The Sentence

The proconsul Saturninus read the decree from the tablet: "Speratus, Nartzalus, Cittinus, Donata, Vestia, Secunda, and the others who confessed that they live after the Christian fashion, since after opportunity was offered them of returning to the Roman way they obstinately persevered, are to be punished by the sword." Speratus said, "We give thanks to God." Nartzalus said, "Today we are martyrs in heaven; thanks be to God." The proconsul Saturninus ordered it announced by a herald: "Speratus, Nartzalus, Cittinus, Veturius, Felix, Aquilinus, Laetantius, Januaria, Generosa, Vestia, Donata, Secunda, have been ordered led out [to execution]." All of them said, "Thanks be to God." And they were immediately beheaded for the name of Christ. Amen.

The Churches of Gaul

28
IRENAEUS OF LYONS[165]

1. *To Florinus On Monarchy* or *That God Is Not the Author of Evil*

Polycarp of Smyrna

To say no more, Florinus, these opinions are not the result of sound judgment; these opinions are not in harmony with the Church, and involve those who adopt them in the greatest impiety; these opinions not even the heretics outside the Church ever dared declare publicly; these opinions the elders before us, who also were disciples of the apostles, did not hand down to you. For when I was still a boy I saw you in lower Asia in the company of Polycarp, faring brilliantly at the imperial court and trying to secure his favor. For I distinctly recall the events of that time better than those of recent years (for what we learn in childhood keeps pace with the growing mind and becomes part of it), so that I can tell the very place where the blessed Polycarp used to sit as he discoursed, his goings out and his comings in, the character of his life, his bodily appearance, the discourses he would address to the multitude, how he would tell of his conversations with John and the others who had seen the Lord; and what the things were which he had heard from them concerning the Lord, his mighty works and his teaching. As having received them from the eyewitnesses of the life of the Logos, Polycarp would declare them entirely in accordance with the Scriptures. I used to listen diligently to these things even then, by the mercy of God which was upon me, noting them down not on papyrus but in my heart. And by the grace of God I constantly meditate upon them faithfully; and I can testify before God that if that blessed and apostolic elder had heard the like [of your opinions] he would have cried aloud and stopped his ears and said, "Good God, for what sort of times have you kept me, that I should endure these things?" and he would have fled the very place where, sitting or standing, he had heard these words. And this can also be shown from the letters which he wrote, whether to the neighboring churches, confirming them, or to some of the brothers, admonishing and exhorting them.[166]

The Quartodeciman Controversy

2–3. *To Victor* [of Rome]. For there is a controversy not only about the day but also about the very manner of the fast. For some think they ought to fast a single day, but others two, others again even more. And in the opinion of others the "day" amounts to forty continuous hours, day and night. And such variety of observance did not begin recently, in our own time, but much earlier under our predecessors, who apparently disregarded strictness and held to a practise that is simple but individual, establishing it for the future. Nonetheless, all of them lived in peace and we also live in peace with one another, and the disagreement about the fast confirms our agreement in the faith.[167]

Toleration at Rome

3. Among these too were the presbyters before Soter, who presided over the church of which you are now the leader—we mean Anicetus and Pius, Hyginus and Telesphorus and Xystus—neither observed it themselves nor permitted those with them to do so. None the less, though they did not observe it themselves they were at peace with the members of the communities where it was observed when the latter came to them. And none were ever expelled because of this course of action but those very elders before you, though they did not observe it, would send the eucharist to members of those communities who observed it. And when the blessed Polycarp stayed at Rome in the time of Anicetus, though they had some trifling disagreements on other matters, they immediately made peace and did not care to quarrel on this subject. Anicetus could not persuade Polycarp not to observe what he had always observed with John the Lord's disciple and the other apostles with whom he consorted; and Polycarp could not persuade Anicetus to observe it, for he said that he ought to hold to the custom of the elders before him. Though such was the situation, they held communion with each other, and in the church Anicetus yielded the eucharist to Polycarp, obviously out of respect. So they parted from each other in peace and the whole church was at peace, both those who observed and those who did not.[168]

The Church of Rome

29
THE MARTYRDOM OF JUSTIN

The *Acts of Justin* are preserved in three forms; we translate the shortest (Recension "A").[169] See H. Musurillo, *The Acts of the Christian Martyrs* ([Oxford: Clarendon, 1972], xviii–xx, 42–47).

Preliminaries

Martyrdom of the holy Justin, Chariton, Charito, Euelpistus, Hierax, Paeon, Liberian, and their company.

In the time of the lawless decrees of idolatry the aforementioned saints were arrested and brought before the prefect of Rome, Rusticus. When they had been brought in, the prefect said to Justin, "What is your way of life?" Justin said, "Blameless and without reproach before all men." Rusticus the prefect said, "What precepts do you profess?" Justin said, "I undertook to learn all precepts, but I adhere to the true precepts of the Christians though they do not please those with false opinions." Rusticus the prefect said, "So those precepts please you?" Justin said, "Yes, since I follow them with the right doctrine." Rusticus the prefect said, "What kind of doctrine?" Justin said, "That we worship the God of the Christians, whom we consider to be one, from the beginning Maker and Creator of the whole creation; and the Son of God Jesus Christ, who was foretold by the prophets as going to come to the human race as herald and teacher of good precepts. I think I can say little compared with his deity, but I acknowledge the power of prophecy, that it was foretold of him whom I named as Son of God. You must know that the prophets spoke from the beginning about his future coming among men."

51

Places of Meeting

Rusticus the prefect said, "Where do you meet?" Justin said, "Where each one chooses and is able. For do you think it possible for us all to come together in the same place?" Rusticus the prefect said, "Tell me, where do you meet or in what place?" Justin said, "I live above the bath of Myrtinus[170] and during all this time (this is my second stay in the city of Rome) I have known no other assembly than the one there. And whoever wanted to come to me, I shared the words of truth with him."

Abandon Christianity

Rusticus said, "Well, finally, you are a Christian?" Justin said, "Yes, I am a Christian." The prefect Rusticus said to Chariton, "Chariton, are you a Christian too?" Chariton said, "I am a Christian, by God's command." Rusticus the prefect said to Charito, "And what do you say, Charito?" Charito said, "I am a Christian, by God's gift." Rusticus the prefect said to Euelpistus, "And who are you?" Euelpistus said, "I too am a Christian, and I share the same hope." Rusticus the prefect said to Hierax, "Are you a Christian?" Hierax said, "Yes, I am a Christian, worshiping the same God." Rusticus the prefect said, "Did Justin make you Christians?" Hierax replied, "I have been a Christian for a long time." Paeon, who was standing by, said, "I too am a Christian." Rusticus said, "Who taught you?" Paeon said, "We received it from our parents." Euelpistus said, "I was glad to hear Justin's discourse, but I too received my Christian training from my parents." Rusticus said, "Where are your parents?" Euelpistus said, "In Cappadocia." Rusticus the prefect said to Hierax, "Where are your parents?" He answered and said, "They are dead, and I was long ago abducted from Phrygia." Rusticus the prefect said to Liberianus, "Are you too a Christian?" Liberianus said, "I too am a devout Christian."

Warnings

The prefect said to Justin, "If you are beaten and beheaded, do you believe you are going to ascend into the sky?" Justin said, "I hope for reward for endurance if I endure. For I know that for those who live rightly, the divine gift of grace is waiting until the final conflagration." Rusticus the prefect said, "So you suppose you will ascend?" Justin said, "I do not suppose so, I am certain of it." Rusticus the prefect said, "If you do not obey you will be punished." Justin said, "We pray that after punishment we will be saved."

The Sentence

Rusticus the prefect declared, "Those who do not want to sacrifice to the gods are to be beaten and led away in conformity with the laws." The holy martyrs, glorifying God, came out to the appointed place and were beheaded, thus perfecting their testimony in the confession of our Savior, to whom be glory and power with the Father and the Holy Spirit, now and for ever. Amen.

Part III

Identifying Heresy

30
JUSTIN AGAINST ALL HERESIES

In the course of his *Apology*, written about 150, the Christian teacher Justin refers to his earlier treatise against all the heresies, and presumably echoes it.

After Christ's ascension into heaven the demons moved certain men to call themselves gods. These were not only not persecuted by you [the emperors] but even deemed worthy of honors. A certain Simon of Samaria, from a village named Gittae, under Claudius Caesar worked magical miracles in your imperial city of Rome through the power of the demons who energized him. He was considered a god and honored as a god among you by a statue on the Tiber river between the two bridges, bearing this inscription in Latin: 'To Simon the Holy God' (*SIMONI SANCTO DEO*).[171] And practically all the Samaritans as well as a few among other races acknowledge and worship him as the First God, and they say that a certain Helena, associated with him at that time though previously a prostitute, became the First Thought from him.

A certain Menander, himself a Samaritan from the village of Kapparetaia, became a disciple of Simon.[172] He too was energized by the demons and came to Antioch, where he led many astray though the art of magic. He persuaded his followers that they would never die; and even now there are some followers of his who acknowledge this.

A certain Marcion of Pontus is even now teaching those who believe him to imagine a God greater than the Creator. By the aid of the demons he made many speak blasphemies and deny God the Creator of this universe and acknowledge another as greater than he.

All who are descended from these are called Christians just as those who do not share the same doctrines among philosophers share the common name of philosophy.

We do not know if they practise those shameful deeds of rumor, the overturn of the lamp and the promiscuous unions and the consumption of human flesh, but we do know that they are neither persecuted nor killed by you even for their doctrines. We have compiled a treatise against all the extant heresies; if you wish to read it we will provide a copy.[173]

31
THE INSCRIPTION "TO SIMON"

Examples of the dedication supposedly "To Simon" occur in inscriptions still extant.

CIL 6 (part 4.2).30994 (ILS 3472) *SACRED TO SEMO SANCUS SANCTUS DEUS FIDIUS* (now in the Vatican Museum).
CIL 6.568 (ILS 3473) *SACRED TO SANCUS SANCTUS SEMO DEUS FIDIUS*
CIL 6.567 (ILS 3474) *SACRED TO SEMO SANCUS DEUS FIDIUS* (from the Tiber Island).[174]

All three inscriptions use an ordinary term (*deus*) for the more obscure *dius*, and two of them apparently explain *sancus* by *sanctus*. We may add that Augustine seems aware of the variant: "The Sabines enrolled their first king Sancus, or, as some call him, Sanctus, among the gods."[175] Or is he combining a statement by Varro with Tertullian's mention of the Simonian inscription *SANCTI DEI*?[176]

32
BASILIDES

Basilides, at Alexandria early in the second century, insisted on the apostolic origin of his teaching, claiming that it came either from "Glaukias the interpreter of Peter" or from Matthias the replacement for Judas.[177] Like his son Isidore he was deeply concerned with free will and ethics.

Suffering the Result of Sin

1. What I mean is that those [like the martyrs] who undergo such tribulations have really sinned unawares and by those other failings are brought to this result. They are accused because of the goodness of their leader but actually on other grounds, so that they may not suffer as men condemned for confessed crimes but because they are not yet Christians though born such by nature. He will console them so that they will not even seem to suffer. If anyone who has not sinned at all comes to suffer—such a case is rare—he will not suffer from the plotting of power, but he will suffer as the infant suffers who seems not to have sinned. The infant has not previously or actively committed any sin, but within himself he has the potential for sinning. When he is subjected to suffering he is benefited even though he reaps many unpleasant results. Just so, even if a perfect man has not sinned in act or by chance but suffers, his suffering corresponds to that of the infant. For within himself he has the capacity for sin, even though, since he did not accept the opportunity to sin, he did not sin. Therefore his not sinning does him no credit. The man who wants to commit adultery is an adulterer even if he does not happen to commit adultery; the man who wants to commit murder is a murderer even if he is unable to murder [cf. Matt. 5:22, 28]. Similarly, if I see the suffering of anyone whom I may call sinless, I shall call his will to sin wicked even if he has done nothing evil. For I will say anything rather than call Providence evil.

What of the Suffering of Jesus?

Now if you disregard all these examples and try to shame me by saying of so and so that he did not sin but he did suffer—if you permit me, I will say that he did not sin but was like the infant who suffers. And if you should press the argument more strenuously, I will say that any man you may name is a man; the just one is God [Mark 10:18; Luke 18:19]. For "no one," as someone said, "is pure from defilement" [Job 14:4].[178]

2. We suppose one part of the declared will of God to be to love all things because all are related to the Whole, and another part, not to desire anything, and a third part, not to hate anything.[179]

3. The apostle said, "I once lived apart from law" [Rom. 7:9], that is, before I came into this body I lived in the kind of body that was not under law, such as that of a beast or a bird.[180]

33
ISIDORE SON OF BASILIDES

On the Indivisible Soul

4. If you give proofs to someone that the soul is not indivisible but that the passions of the wicked come from the force of the "appendages" (*prosarté-mata*), then worthless men are given no slight pretext to say, "I was forced, I was carried away, I did it unwillingly, I acted against my will" [cf. Rom. 7:15–20]. But the man himself is in control of his desire for evil things and is not fighting the force of the "appendages." We must gain superiority by our rational faculty and show ourselves overpowering the inferior creature [cf. Gen. 1:28; Rom. 7:23–25] within us.[181]

Expositions of the Prophet Parchor

5. Attic philosophers say that certain matters were intimated to Socrates by an attendant spirit [*daimôn*]. And Aristotle says that all men are provided with spirits which attend them while they are in the body.[182] He takes this teaching from the prophets and transfers it to his own books without acknowledging the source of the statement. . . . No one should suppose that what we call peculiar to the elect was spoken previously by any of the philosophers. For it was not their discovery; they appropriated it from the prophets and attributed it to some "wise man"—who according to them does not exist. . . . It seems to me that those who philosophize do so in order to learn what the "winged oak" is, and what the "cloak embroidered on it" is, all of which Pherecydes used as theological allegories after taking the idea from the *Prophecy of Ham*.[183]

Ethics

6. When the apostles asked whether it was better not to marry, the Lord answered, "Not all can keep this saying, for some are eunuchs from birth, others from necessity" [Matt. 19:11–12].[184] Some have from birth a natural aversion to women, and they make right use of this natural constitution by not marrying. These are the eunuchs "from birth." Those "from necessity" are continent for the sake of theatrical contests; they control themselves because of the attraction given by approval. These, then, become eunuchs in accordance with necessity, not reason. But those who make themselves eunuchs because of the eternal kingdom [Matt. 19:12]

choose this course because of the consequences of marriage, fearing that they will lack leisure [cf. 1 Cor. 7:5] because they will have to earn money.

The apostle said, "It is better to marry than to burn" [1 Cor. 7:9] lest you cast your soul into the fire while you resist night and day and are afraid of falling away from continence. While the soul resists, it is separated from hope.

Therefore avoid a "contentious woman" [Prov. 21:9, 19] so that you will not be torn away from the grace of God. After emitting the seed of "fire," pray with a good conscience. But when your prayer of thanksgiving declines into petition, and you ask, for the future, not to be reformed but to fall, then marry. But if someone is a youth or a pauper or impotent, and he does not wish to marry in accordance with this word, he must not be separated from his brother. He is to say, "I have entered into the Holy of Holies and I cannot experience passion." But if he has a suspicion [that he may fall], he is to say, "Brother, lay your hand on me so that I will not sin." He will get help in mind and sense. He must only wish to attain what is good, and he will attain it.

Sometimes we say with our mouth, "We do not wish to sin, but the notion of sin is in my mind." Such a person does not do what he wishes simply because of fear that punishment will be put to his account. But mankind has certain needs that are both necessary and natural, others that are only natural. The need of clothing is necessary and natural, while the need of sexual intercourse is natural but not necessary.[185]

34
VALENTINUS

Valentinus taught, perhaps at Rome, before the middle of the second century. He relied on older mythology but, like his major disciples, used exegesis for relating it to the Christian books.

Origin of His Heresy according to Hippolytus

Valentinus saw a newborn infant [see Fragment 7] and asked him who he was. He replied that he was the Logos. Valentinus then added some "tragic myth" and wanted the heresy he was promoting to consist of this.[186]

Letters

1. Something like fear of this creature [man] fell upon the angels, for he made utterances greater than were suitable for his creation because of the

One who had invisibly put in him the seed of the substance from above— the One who expresses himself freely. So also among the generations of earthly men, the works of men became terrors for them, as in the case of statues and images and everything which [human] hands fashion in the name of a god. So Adam, fashioned in the name of a man, inspired the fear attaching to the preexistent Man, as if this Man had his existence in him. The angels were terrified and rapidly spoiled the work.[187]

2. The Good is one [Matt. 19:17]. His presence is the manifestation through the Son. By him alone can the heart become pure [Matt. 5:9] when every evil spirit is expelled from the heart. For many spirits dwelling in it do not allow it to be pure; each of them performs its own works, assaulting it with unseemly desires in many ways.

It seems to me that the heart suffers rather as an inn does. An inn has holes and trenches dug in it and often is filled with dung by men who stay there, behaving licentiously and taking no care of the place because it belongs to someone else.[188] Just so, the heart is unclean before it is cared for; it is the abode of many demons. But when the Father, who alone is good, visits it, it is sanctified and shines with light. Thus he who has such a heart is "blessed, because he will see God" [Matt. 5:8].[189]

3. While he endured everything, he was continent. Jesus exercised his divine nature. He ate and drank in a peculiar way [cf. Matt. 11:19] and did not evacuate his food. For he had so great a power of continence that the food was not corrupted in him, since he himself was not perishable.[190]

Homilies

4. From the very beginning you are immortal and children of eternal life. You wished to distribute death among yourselves in order to consume it and spend it, so that death might die in you and through you. For when you destroy the world but are not destroyed yourselves, you are lords over the creation [cf. Gen. 1:28] and over all decay.[191]

5. The world is as much inferior to the living Aeon as the image is to the living person. What then is the cause of the image? It is the greatness of the person who provides the model for the painter, so that it may be honored by his name. For even though the authenticity of the form is not found [in the image], the name supplies what is lacking in the work. The invisible power of God works with the creation so that we may believe that the creation is his.[192]

6. Many things written in the ordinary books are also written in the Church of God. For they are common words from the heart, the law written in the heart [Jer. 31:33]. This is the people of the Beloved, loved by him and loving him.[193]

Harvest

> 7. In spirit I see all things suspended,
> in spirit I perceive all things borne up,
> flesh suspended from soul,
> soul borne up by air,
> air hanging from ether.
> Out of the deep, fruits being borne;
> out of the womb, a child is born.[194]

35
PTOLEMAEUS
ON THE OLD TESTAMENT LAW

I include the *Letter to Flora* by the Valentinian Gnostic Ptolemaeus[195] because much of it is close to the Christian critical orthodoxy of his time. I have suggested elsewhere that "Flora" is not an individual but the "hieratic" name of the city of Rome.[196]

Errors about the Law

Many do not understand the Law ordained through Moses, my good sister Flora, since they know neither the one who ordained it nor its exact commandments, but I think it will readily become clear to you if you learn the varying opinions about it. There are those who say it was decreed by God the Father; others, on the contrary, assert that it was ordained by the hostile and corrupting Devil, to whom they attribute the creation of the world, calling him the father and creator of this universe. But those who recite this to one another are quite wrong, and in both ways they go astray from the evident truth. For it is clear that the Law, which is secondary, was not ordained by the perfect God and Father, since it is imperfect, lacks completion [by Christ], and contains commandments alien to the nature and purpose of such a God. Again, the Law cannot be attributed to the injustice of the Adversary, for it is opposed to injustice. Both of these opinions follow from not attending to what was said by the Savior. For "a house divided against itself cannot stand" [Matt. 12:25], our Savior declared. Furthermore, the Apostle, refuting the inconsistent wisdom of these liars, says the creation of the world was his: "All things were made through him, and apart from him was made nothing" [John 1:1]. It was the creation not of a death-dealing god but of a just one who hates evil. Theirs is the opinion of heedless men who do not understand the cause of the providence of the Demiurge, men who are blind not only in the eye of the soul but also in that of the body. How they have strayed from the truth is clear to you from what has been said. Two groups have introduced their own views, some through not knowing the God of justice, others through not knowing the Father of All, whom only he who alone knew him revealed at his coming [Matt. 11:27].

Now it remains for us to consider the opinions of both of these and to explain and clarify the Law to you, what its nature is, and by whom it was given, the Lawgiver, proving our demonstrations from the words of our Savior, through which alone we can pass without error to the comprehension of reality.

Three Sources of the Pentateuchal Law

First, you must know that the whole Law contained in the Pentateuch was not decreed by one person, I mean God, alone; but there are also some decrees in it ordained by men. The words of the Savior teach us that it is tripartite. One part is ascribed to God himself and his legislation; another is ascribed to Moses, not as God gave the Law through him but as Moses legislated some elements from his own understanding; and the third is ascribed to the elders of the people, who are found first introducing certain ordinances of their own. You may learn from the words of the Savior how this is so. When the Savior was once conversing with those who came to question him about divorce, which the Law permitted, he said to them, "Moses for the hardness of your hearts permitted a man to put away his wife; from the beginning it was not so" [Matt. 19:8]. For God made this union, he said, and what God has united, "let no man put asunder" [19:6]. Here he shows that the Law of God is one thing, forbidding a woman to be divorced by her husband, and the law of Moses is another, permitting the breaking of the bond because of hardness of heart. Then in this matter Moses ordains a law contrary to God, for divorce is contrary to no divorce.

But if we carefully examine the purpose of Moses, according to which he made this law, we find that he did not do this on his own account but of necessity because the weakness of those for whom he legislated. For since they could not achieve the will of God, who forbids them to divorce their wives (with whom some of them lived incompatibly), they stood in danger of falling into greater wrongdoing and from this into annihilation. Desiring to free them from this dreadful situation through which they might have perished, Moses substituted a second law for the critical times, a lesser for a greater, and of his own accord decreed the law of divorce for them so that if they could not keep the other and yet could keep this they might not fall into injustice and evil, which would have led them to total destruction. This was his opinion, in which he is found to be legislating against God. It is beyond doubt that this law of Moses was different from the Law of God, if we have proved it only through one example.

Now the Savior also makes clear that there are some traditions of the elders bound up with the Law. For "God said, Honor your father and your mother, that it may be well with you. But you call"—addressing the elders—"a gift to God whatever might have profited you from me, and you make void the Law of God by the tradition of your elders" [Matt. 15:4–6]. "Isaiah also cried out, saying, 'This people honors me with their lips, but their heart is far from me. They worship me in vain, teaching as their doctrines the precepts of men'" [7–9]. Clearly, then, the whole Law is proved from these examples to be divided into three parts: we find in it the legislation of Moses himself and of the elders and of God. And here this division of the whole Law shows its own truth to us.

Three Sources of the Law of God

Again, that part of the Law which is from God himself is divided into three parts: (1) into pure legislation, free from evil, which is rightly called Law and which the Savior "came not to destroy but to complete" [Matt. 5:17] (for that which he fulfilled was not alien from him, or it could not have been perfected); and (2) into that part bound up with lower things and injustice, a law which the Savior abrogated as alien to his own nature; and it is divided also (3) into that part which is typical and symbolical, legislated as images of spiritual and better things, which the Savior transformed from the sensible and phenomenal into the spiritual and invisible.

The Pure Legislation

And that pure Law of God free from evil is none other than the Decalogue, those ten sentences divided into two tablets, for the prohibition of things not to be done and the injunction of things to be done. Though they are pure legislation they do not reach perfection, for they lacked completion by the Savior.

The Inadequate Law

The second kind, bound up with wrongdoing and concerned with vengeance and retribution for previous wrongs, contains and commands payment of "an eye for an eye and a tooth for a tooth and a death for a death" [Deut. 19:21; cf. Matt. 5:38]. For the second wrongdoer is not less unjust; he differs only in sequence while he does the same deed. But this commandment was and is just, ordained because of the weakness of those for whom the legislation was made. It was intended to avoid transgression of the pure Law, but it is alien to the nature and goodness of the Father of all. It resulted from adaptation to circumstances, or rather from necessity. For when he who forbids a single murder, saying, "Thou shalt not kill" [Matt. 5:22], ordered the murderer to be murdered, laid down a second law, and commanded a double murder (he who had forbidden one), he forgot himself, overwhelmed by necessity. Therefore the Son sent by him took away that part of the law, though he admitted it was from God, both in those parts ascribed to the ancient sect [Judaism] and in those in which God had spoken, saying, "He who curses father or mother shall surely die" [Exod. 21:17].

The Law with Images and Symbols

Then there is the third part of it, which is "typical," in the likeness of spiritual and better things, namely, on sacrifice and circumcision and Sabbath and fasting and Passover and unleavened bread, and legislation on [other] such matters. All these things, being images and symbols, were transformed when the truth was made manifest. The material performance according to appearance was taken away, but revealed according to what is spiritual. The names remained the same but the deeds were different. For the Savior commanded us to offer sacrifices, but not of irrational animals or incense but of spiritual praises and gloryings and thanksgiving, and through fellowship and beneficence toward neighbors. And he wants us to be circumcised, not by the material circumcision of the foreskin but by the spiritual circumcision of the heart; and to keep the Sabbath, for he wants us to keep away from evil deeds; and to fast, but he wants us to keep not a bodily fast but a spiritual one, in which there is an avoidance of all bad things. But indeed our people should also keep the outward fast, since it may bring something to the soul when it is done with reason and not in imitation of others or for custom or because of a day as if appointed for this purpose; but as a reminder of the true fast, so that those who are not able to keep that may have a reminder of it through the outward fast. And similarly the apostle Paul shows that the Passover and the unleavened bread are images, saying, "Christ our Passover has been sacrificed," and he continued, "so that you may be unleavened, not having leaven" (by "leaven" he means evil) "but may be new dough" [1 Cor. 5:7–8].

The Savior and the Law of God

Thus the Law of God is divided into three parts: into the part completed by the Savior, for the "Thou shalt not kill, thou shalt not commit adultery, thou shall not swear falsely" was fulfilled in the commandment not to be angry nor to lust nor to swear an oath. Another part was that taken away completely; for "An eye for an eye and a tooth for a tooth," bound up with wrongdoing and itself containing the word of injustice, was taken away by the Savior through its opposite (opposites are destructive of each other). "For I say to you, resist not evil, but if anyone strikes you, turn the other cheek also to him" [Matt. 5:39]. Now the symbolical part is allegorical of what is transformed and changed from bodily into spiritual; it was given as law as an image of the things above. For the images and symbols were good, in so far as they were representative of other things, as long as the truth had not yet appeared; but when the truth appears, one must do the deeds of the truth, not those of the image. His disciples and the Apostle showed these things, exhibiting for us the image-part of the law, as we have already said, by the Passover and the unleavened bread; the part of the law bound up with wrongdoing, in the saying "The abolition of the law of commandments contained in ordinances" [Eph. 2:15]; and finally the part not connected with inferior things, in the saying "The Law is holy and the commandment holy and just and good" [Rom. 7:12].

What God Gave the Law?

In short, then, I think I have sufficiently shown you both the legislation introduced by men and the threefold division of the Law of God. There remains for us the question, Who is this God who gave the Law? I think this also has been shown you from the preceding remarks, if you have paid close attention. For if the Law was given neither by the perfect God himself, as we have taught, nor by the Devil, a thing which it is not right to say, someone other than these two must have given the Law. And he is the Demiurge and creator of this whole world and what is in it, and he is different from the nature of those two; standing as a mediator between them, he should rightly bear the name "the Middle."[197] And if that perfect God is good by his nature, as he is ("For one only is the good God" [Matt. 19:17], our Savior said of his Father whom he revealed), and if the evil and wickedness of the Adversary's nature is characterized by injustice, then he who stands between them as a mediator, and is neither good nor bad nor unjust, may correctly be called just, since he is the bearer of justice. And this god will be lower than the perfect God and less than his justice, for indeed he is also begotten and not unbegotten—for "one" is the unbegotten "Father, from whom is everything" [Eph. 3:14, cf. 4:6] since everything was fashioned by him, but he will become greater and more powerful than the Adversary, and will have a different nature and essence from the other two. But the nature of the Adversary is corruption and darkness, for he is material and divided into many parts. The nature of the unbegotten Father of everything is incorruption and self-sufficient light, single and uniform. The nature of this God has brought forth two powers. . . . He himself, however, is an image of the higher one.

Do not let this disturb you now in your desire to learn how from one Beginning of everything, which we confess and believe, unbegotten and incorrupt and good, there came these two natures, one of corruption and one of the Middle, both entirely different in nature, though the good one has the ability to beget and bring forth things like itself and of the same nature. For with God's help you will learn in order the beginning and the begetting of this, if you are deemed worthy of the apostolic tradition which we too have received from a succession together with the regulation of all our words by the teaching of the Savior. I have placed these matters before you, my dear sister Flora, in few words, and I have written them down as a short summary—yet I have handled the question adequately. And it will be highly advantageous to you in the future if through this discussion you will bring forth fruit as a good and fertile land is productive by means of potent seeds.[198]

On the Prologue of John

When John the Lord's disciple wants to tell of the origin of the universe, by which the Father produced everything, he posits a certain Beginning first generated by God, which he calls Only-Begotten Son and God, in which the Father spermatically emitted all things. By this the Logos was emitted, and in it was the whole substance of the Aeons, which the Logos itself later shaped. Since, then, he speaks of the first origin, he rightly sets forth the teaching from the Beginning, that is, God and the Logos; for he says, "In the Beginning was the Logos, and the Logos was with God, and the Logos was God; this was in the Beginning with God" [John 1:1–2]. First he differentiates the three: God, Beginning, and Logos; then he combines them again in order to set forth the emission of each of them, the

Son and the Logos, and their unity with each other and with the Father. For in the Father and from the Father is the Beginning, and in the Beginning and from the Beginning is the Logos. Rightly, then, he said, "In the Beginning was the Logos," for it was in the Son; and "the Logos was with God," for the Beginning was; and "the Logos was God;" this follows, for what is generated of God is God [cf. John 3:6]. "This was in the Beginning with God": he set forth the order of emission. "All things came into existence through it, and apart from it nothing came into existence" [John 1:3]: the Logos was the cause of formation and origin to all the Aeons after it. "What came into existence in it is Life" [John 1:4]: from this he reveals the Pair [*syzygy*], for "all things" came into existence "through" it, but Life, "in" it. This, then, coming into existence "in" it, is closer "in" it than the things which came into existence "through" it; for it is present "with" it and bears fruit "through" it, since he adds, "And the Life was the Light of Men" [John 1:4]. Having just said "Man," he mentioned "Church" as having the same meaning as "Man," so that through the one name he might set forth the common nature of the Pair; for from Logos and Life come Man and Church. He spoke of Life as the Light of men because they are illuminated by it, that is, transfigured and made manifest. This is what Paul says: "For everything made manifest is Light" [Eph. 5:13]. Since, then, Life manifested and generated Man and Church; it is called their Light.

Clearly, then, through these words John explained, in addition to other matters, the second Tetrad: Logos and Life, Man and Church. Moreover, he revealed the first Tetrad. Discussing the subject of the Savior, and saying that "everything" outside the Pleroma was formed through him, he says that he is the fruit of the whole Pleroma. For he called him the Light shining in the Darkness and not overcome by it [John 1:5], since even when he shaped everything that came into existence out of passion he was not known by it. And he calls him Son and Truth and Life and Incarnate Logos, "whose glory we beheld, and his glory was such as belongs to the Only-Begotten, given him by the Father, full of Grace and Truth" [John 1:14]. He speaks thus: "And the Logos became incarnate and dwelt in us and we beheld his glory, glory as of the Only-Begotten of the Father, full [*plérés*] of Grace and Truth."

Correctly, then, he revealed the first Tetrad, mentioning Father and Grace and Only-Begotten, and Truth. Thus John spoke about the first Ogdoad, the Mother of all the Aeons, for he spoke of Father and Grace and Only-Begotten and Truth and Logos and Life and Man and Church.[199]

36
HERACLEON

Like Ptolemaeus, Heracleon was a leading disciple of Valentinus and taught in "the West," presumably at Rome, in the third quarter of the second century. Origen referred to his comments on John 1–8.

Fragments on John from Origen

The Logos in the Creation

1. [John 1:3: "All things were made through him."] Heracleon limits "all things" to the world and the things in it. "Neither the Aeon nor the things in the Aeon were made through the Logos, but before the Logos existed." ["Without him was nothing made."] He joins "nothing" with "of the things in the world and the creation." The Logos, who provided the cause of the creation of the world to the Demiurge, is not the one "from whom" or "by whom" but the one "through whom." The Logos did not make the world as if energized by another (understanding "through him" thus), but while he himself energized, another made it.[200]

2. [John 1:4: "In him was life."] In spiritual men, for he provided the first formation for them at their birth, guiding and displaying the seeds sown by another into form and illumination and their own outline.[201]

John the Baptist

3. [John 1:18: "No one has ever seen God."] Spoken not by [John] the Baptist but by the disciple.[202]

4. [John 1:20–21: John confessed he was not the Christ or even a prophet or Elijah.[203]]

5. [John 1:23: "I am the voice of one crying in the wilderness."] The Logos is the Savior; the voice in the wilderness is what was represented by John; the sound is the whole prophetic order. The voice well suited for speech becomes speech [*logos*], just as if a woman were to change into a man. And for the sound there will be a change into voice, giving the place of a disciple to the voice transformed into a word, but of a slave to that transformed from sound into voice. When the Savior calls John "prophet" and "Elijah" he does not teach of him but of his circumstances; but when the Savior calls him "greater than prophets" and "among those born of women" [Luke 7:26, 28], then he characterizes John. For when John is asked about himself he answers

about himself, not about his surroundings. His surroundings were, so to speak, his apparel, different from himself, and when he was asked about his apparel, as if he himself were his apparel, he could not answer Yes. [1:19: priests and Levites] It was the business of such persons, devoted to the service of God, to occupy themselves and make inquiries about such matters; furthermore, John was of the Levitical tribe. They asked him if he were a prophet, desiring to know this rather general fact.[204]

6. [John 1:25: "Why are you baptizing if you are not the Christ or Elijah or the prophet?"] Only they have the office to baptize. [What prophet?] The Pharisees inquired from malice, not from a desire to learn.[205]

7. [John 1:26–27: "I baptize with water; but among you stands one whom you do not know, even he who comes after me, the thong of whose sandal I am not worthy to untie."] John answers those sent by the Pharisees, not answering what they asked but saying what he wanted to, forgetting that he accuses the prophet of ignorance, if indeed when asked one thing he replies about another. For this must be regarded as a failure in communication.[206]

8. [John 1:26: "In the midst of you."] He is already present and is in the world and in man and is already manifest to all of you. [1:27: " . . . the thong of whose sandal I am not worthy to untie."] The Baptist confesses through these words that he is not worthy of even the least honorable service for Christ. "I am not worthy that for my sake he should come down from the Greatness and take on flesh as a shoe." I cannot give an account of this flesh or interpret it or explain the divine plan concerning it. All these things must also be understood concerning that person [the Demiurge] represented by John. The Demiurge of the world, inferior to Christ, confesses this through these expressions. The whole world is the "shoe" of Jesus.[207]

9. [John 1:28: "This took place in Bethany."] In Heracleon we read "Bethany."[208]

10. [John 1:29: "Behold the Lamb of God, who takes away the sin of the world."] "Lamb of God" is said by John as a prophet. The first thing is said about his body, the second about the one who was in the body; for as the lamb is imperfect among the genus of sheep, so also is the body in comparison with him who dwells in it. If he had wanted to indicate by the body what is perfect he would have said the ram, which was going to be sacrificed.[209]

Another "Economy" or Divine Plan

11. [John 2:12: "After this he went down to Capernaum."] This again shows the beginning of another divine plan, since "He went down" was not said idly: "Capernaum" signifies these limits of the world, these material

things to which he went down; and because the place was not suitable he is not said to have done or spoken anything there.[210] [See Fragment 13.]

12. [John 2:13: "The Pascha of the Jews was at hand."] This is the great feast; for it was a model for the suffering of the Savior, when not only was the sheep slain but when eaten it afforded repose and when sacrificed it signified the suffering of the Savior in the world and when eaten it signi-fied the repose in marriage.[211]

13. [John 2:13: "Jesus went up to Jerusalem."] The going up to Jerusalem signifies the journey from the material to the place of living things, which is an image of Jerusalem. The words are "He found [sellers] in the temple" and not "in the court of the temple," so that we may under-stand that a calling without the Spirit is not assisted by the Lord. The "tem-ple" is the Holy of Holies, which only the high priest enters [Heb. 9:7], where the spiritual ones go; the court of the temple where the Levites also enter is a symbol of those animate beings who are saved outside the Pleroma. Those who are found "in the temple selling oxen and sheep and doves, and the money changers sitting" represent those who attribute noth-ing to grace but regard the visits of strangers to the temple as a matter of trade and gain, and minister the sacrifices for the worship of God with a view to their own gain and love of money. And the "scourge" which Jesus made "of small cords" is an image of the power and energy of the Holy Spirit, driving out the wicked by his breath. The "scourge" and the linen [Rev. 15:6] and the napkin [Matt. 27:59] and other such things are images of the power and energy of the Holy Spirit. The "scourge" was tied to a piece of wood, which was a type of the cross; on this wood the gamblers, traders, and all evil were nailed up [Col. 2:14] and destroyed. He did not make it of dead leather, for he desired to make the Church no longer a "den of robbers" and traders, but the house of his Father.[212]

14. [John 2:17: "Zeal for your house shall consume me."] Spoken in the person of those powers which were cast out and destroyed by the Savior.[213]

15. [John 2:19: "In three days I will raise it up."] Heracleon reads "In three days" instead of "On the third day." He calls the third "the day of spirit, on which is the resurrection of the Church, for the first is the day of earth and the second the day of soul, and the resurrection of the Church does not take place on these."[214]

16. [John 2:20: "It has taken forty-six years to build this temple."] Solomon building the temple for forty-six years is an image of the Savior; the number six refers to matter, that is, what is formed; the forty, which is a tetrad and is not to be combined [with the six], refers to the inspiration of the Spirit and the seed in the inspiration.[215]

The Samaritan Woman

17. [John 4:14] That fountain means feeble, short, and deficient life, like its glory, for it was worldly. It was worldly because the flocks of Jacob had drunk from it. The water which the Savior gave is from his spirit and his power. "You shall never thirst": for his life is eternal and never corruptible like the first from the well, but permanent. For the grace and the gift of our Savior are not to be taken away or spent or corrupted by the one who shares it. "Springing water": those who accepted the riches supplied from above, poured forth themselves the things supplied to them for the eternal life of others. Without doubting, the Samaritan woman accepted a faith corresponding to her nature, and did not hesitate over what he said to her. "Give me this water": aroused by his short speech she hated even the place of that so-called living water. The woman said these things to show the toilsome and laborious and ill-nutritious quality of that water.[216]

18. [John 4:16: "Go, call your husband and come here."] It is clear that this means, If you wish to receive this water, "go, call your husband"; the man whom the Savior calls the woman's husband is her Pleroma, so that coming with him to the Savior she might receive from him power and union and mixture with her Pleroma; for Christ did not tell the woman to call her earthly husband, since he was not unaware that she had no lawful husband. The Savior said to her, "Call your husband and come here," meaning her companion from the Pleroma. [4:17: "You said truly that you had no husband."] Since in the world the Samaritan woman had no husband, for her husband was in the Aeon. [4:18: "You have had five husbands and he whom you now have is not your husband."] The "six husbands" signify all material evil, to which she was bound and tied when she fornicated irrationally and was insulted and abandoned and slighted by them.[217]

19. [John 4:19: "I see that you are a prophet."] In proper fashion the Samaritan woman admitted the things he said to her, for only a prophet knows everything. The Samaritan woman acted in accord with her nature, neither lying nor openly confessing her immorality. Persuaded that he was a prophet, she asked him, also revealing the cause of her fornication, which was due to ignorance of God and God's worship and care for the necessities of life . . . for she would not have come to the well, which was outside the city, unless she had desired to learn in what way and by pleasing whom, she might turn away from fornication by the worship of God. Therefore she says, "Our fathers worshiped in this mountain" [4:20].[218]

20. [John 4:21: "Believe me, woman, for the hour is coming when neither on this mountain nor in Jerusalem will you worship the Father."] At

first Jesus did not say to her, "Believe me, woman," but now he addresses her thus. The "mountain" means the Devil, or his world, since the Devil was a part of the whole of matter, and the whole world is a mountain of evil, a desert inhabited by wild beasts [cf. Mark 1:13], which all those under the Law and all the gentiles worship; "Jerusalem" is the creator whom the Jews adore. But you as spirituals "will worship" neither the creation nor the Demiurge but the "Father" of truth. He receives her as already a believer and one counted with those who "worship in truth" [4:23].[219]

21. [John 4:22: "You worship what you do not know."] Heracleon understands "you" as the Jews [and] the gentiles. He quotes the *Preaching of Peter*: "We must not worship in Greek fashion, accepting the works of matter and adoring wood and stone; nor in Jewish fashion worship the divine, since they, thinking that they alone know him, do not know him and worship angels and the month and the moon."[220]

22. [John 4:22: "We worship what we know, for salvation is from the Jews."] We worship the one in the Aeon and those who come with him; for these knew the one they worship, worshiping in truth. "Salvation is from the Jews": because from that race salvation and the Logos have come to the world; spiritually, salvation is from the Jews, since they are considered images of the beings in the Pleroma.

[John 4:24: "In spirit and in truth. . . ."] Formerly the worshipers worshiped in flesh and error one who is not the Father, so that they were all in error as worshipers of the Demiurge. "They worshiped the creation" [Rom. 1:25] and not the true Creator, who is Christ, since "all things were made through him and apart from him nothing was made" [John 1:3].[222]

23. [John 4:23] That [divine element] related to the Father has been lost in the abysmal matter of error, and is being sought so that the Father may be worshiped by his own. Heracleon's disciples also speak of "the lost spiritual nature" and the "times or ages before its destruction."[221]

24. [John 4:24: "God is a spirit, and those who worship must worship in spirit and truth."] His divine nature is undefiled and pure and invisible. He is rightly worshiped in a spiritual not carnal manner, for those who are of the same nature as the Father are "spirit," who worship in truth and not in error, according to the religion that the Apostle taught, calling it "divine service" [Rom. 12:1]. Heracleon says some are "fallen; the Samaritan woman, whose nature was spiritual, committed fornication."[223]

25. [John 4:25: "I know that Messiah is coming; when he comes he will show us all things."] The Church received Christ and believed of him that he alone knows all things.[224]

26. [John 4:26–27] Since the Samaritan woman believed of Christ that at his coming he would tell her everything, he says, "Know that I who speak to you am he whom you expect"; and when he confessed that he had come as the expected one, "his disciples came to him," and on their account he went into Samaria.[225]

27. [John 4:28: "The woman left her waterpot and went away to the city."] The "waterpot" is the condition and thought capable of receiving life and power from the Savior. They are left behind him, that is, they have such a vessel from the Savior as that with which she came to take the living water, and went away into the world to proclaim the presence of Christ at his call. For the soul is drawn to the Savior through the Spirit and by the Spirit. [John 4:30] "They went out of the city": Out of their first way of life, which was worldly; and they came through faith to the Savior.[226]

28. [John 4:31: "The disciples asked him, saying Rabbi, eat."] They wanted to share with him what they had bought [4:8] and brought from Samaria.[227]

29. [John 4:32: "I have food to eat which you do not know."] Heracleon says nothing on this passage.[228]

30. [John 4:33: "Did anyone bring anything for him to eat?"] These things were spoken carnally by the disciples, "who thinking even more poorly imitate the Samaritan woman, who said, 'You have no dipper and the well is deep'" [4:11].[229]

31. [John 4:34: "My food is that I may do the will of him who sent me."] The Savior explained to the disciples that this was what he discussed with the woman calling the "will" of the Father his own food, for this was his food and repose and power. The "will" of the Father is for men to know the Father and be saved. This was the Savior's work because of which he was sent into Samaria, that is, into the world.[230]

Sowing and Reaping

32. [John 4:35ff.] He speaks of the harvest of the fruits as if this had a fixed period of four months and were already at hand. The harvest means the souls of believers; they are already ripe and ready for harvest and suitable for gathering into the barn, that is, through faith into repose—some are ready but not all. Some were already ready, but some were about to be; those about to be are already sown.[231]

33. [John 4:37: "One sows, another reaps."] This means the same as "The harvest is great and the workers are few" [Matt. 9:37], for they are

ready for harvest and suitable for gathering into the barn through faith into repose [repeated from Frag. 32], and suited for salvation and the reception of the word, because of their creation and nature.[232]

34. [John 4:36: "The reaper receives a wage."] Since the Savior calls himself the reaper, the wage of our Lord is the salvation and restoration of the reaped ones, that he may repose in them.[233]

35. [John 4:36: "The sower rejoices along with the reaper."] For the sower rejoices because he sows and because some of his seeds have already come together, having the same hope also about the others; and he who reaps likewise reaps something. But the first, who sows, began the work and the second reaps. Both cannot begin at the same time; for first it must be sowed, then reaped. When the sower stops sowing, then the reaper reaps. At the present time, both having done their own tasks rejoice together, having the ripening of the seeds as a common joy. [John 4:37: "In this the saying is true that one sows, another reaps."] For the Son of Man above the Place sows [cf. Matt. 13:37], but the Savior, who is also himself Son of Man, reaps and sends reapers, no doubt those who the disciples thought were angels, each for his own soul.[234]

36. [John 4:36: "The sower rejoices with the reaper."] Not through them or by them—the apostles—were these seeds sown, but "those who labored" are the angels of the divine plan, through whom as mediators they were sown and nourished. "You entered into their labors" [John 4:38]: The labor of sowers and reapers is not the same, for the former sow, ploughing the ground in cold and wet and toil, and throughout the winter care for it by digging; but the latter, entering upon a prepared crop, joyfully reap the harvest.[235]

Samaria

37. [John 4:39: "Many Samaritans from that city believed in him because of the woman's word."] "From that city" means "from the world." "Because of the woman's word" means "through the spiritual Church." The "many" are the psychics, for the one nature of [spiritual] election is incorruptible and uniform and unique.[236]

38. [John 4:40: "He stayed there for two days."] He stayed with them and not in them; and the "two days" doubtless [means] the present age and the future time of marriage; or the time before his suffering and after the suffering, the time which he passed with them, turning many more to faith by his own word [4:41], and after which he was separated from them [4:42].[237]

39. [John 4:42: "We no longer believe through your word, for we ourselves have heard and know that he is [truly] the Savior of the world."]
Heracleon says that the word "alone" is lacking and says, "For men first
believe in the Savior after instruction by men; but when they encounter his
words they no longer believe through human testimony alone but through
the truth itself."[238]

The Official's Son at Capernaum

40. [John 4:46–54: "There was an official whose son was ill in Capernaum."] The "official" (*basilikon*) is the Demiurge, since he is a king over
those under him. Because his kingdom is small and temporary he was
called an official, like some petty king appointed by a universal king over
a small kingdom. His son "in Capernaum" is in the lower, intermediate
area by the sea, that is, adjoining to matter. The son of this man is sick,
that is, is not acting according to nature, but is in ignorance and sins.
"From Judaea to Galilee" [4:47] means from the Judaea above. "He was
going to die" overthrows the opinions of those who suppose the soul is
immortal; "soul and body are destroyed in Gehenna" [Matt. 10:28]. The
soul is not immortal but only suited for salvation; the "corruptible put on
incorruption and the mortal put on immortality" when the "death" of the
soul was "swallowed up in victory" [1 Cor. 15:53–55]. "If you do not see
signs and wonders you do not believe" [John 4:48] is suitably addressed
to such a person as through works and sense-perception has the nature to
obey, not through reason the nature to believe. "Come down before my
son dies" [John 4:49] means that death is the purpose of Law [Rom. 7:13],
which kills through sins. Therefore before he had altogether died on
account of his sins, the father asked the Savior alone to help his son, that
is, a nature of this kind. "Your son lives" [4:50], the Savior said through
modesty, since he did not say, "Let him live," nor did he show that he himself provided life. Going down to the sick man and healing him of the dis-
ease, that is, of sins, and by this remission making him alive, he said,
"Your son lives." The man "believed" [4:53]: the Demiurge can easily
believe that the Savior can heal even at a distance. "Slaves of the officer"
[John 4:51] are the angels of the Demiurge, announced in the words "Your
child lives," which is most suitable. Therefore the slaves announced to the
officer what pertained to the salvation of his son, since the angels first look
on the deeds of men in the world to see if they have lived in health and
authenticity since the sojourn of the Savior. "The seventh hour" [4:52]:
By the "hour" is characterized the nature of the one healed. "He and his

whole house believed" [4:53]: This means the angelic order, and the men more closely related to it. It was a question whether certain angels were saved, those who came down to the "daughters of men" [Gen. 6:2]. The destruction of the men of the Demiurge is shown by "The sons of the kingdom will come into outer darkness" [Matt. 8:12]. Concerning this Isaiah prophesied: "I begot sons and raised them up; but they spurned me" [Isa. 1:2, 4]—they are alien sons and an evil seed and lawless and makers of a vine of thorns [cf. Isa. 5:2].[239]

Controversy between Jesus and the Jews

41. [John 8:21: "Where I go you cannot come."] How, being in ignorance and unbelief and sins, can they come to be in incorruption?[240]

42. [John 8:22: "The Jews said, 'Will he kill himself?'"] The Jews thought wickedly when they said these things and presumed themselves to be greater than the Savior, and supposed that they would go to God for eternal repose while the Savior went to corruption and death, slaying himself, where they did not think they would go. The Jews thought the Savior said, "I having slain myself am going to corruption, where you cannot come."[241]

43. [John 8:37: "My word does not abide in you."] It does not "abide," for the reason that they are unfit, whether by nature or by inclination.[242]

44. [John 8:43–44: "Why do you not know my speech? Because you cannot hear my word. You are of your father the Devil."] A reason is given for their not "being able to hear" the words of Jesus nor know his word, in the "You are of your father the Devil." Why "can you not hear my word?" Is it not that "You are of your father the Devil" means of the nature of the Devil? This makes their nature clear to them and judges them, for they are neither children of Abraham, for they would not have hated him, nor children of God, because they did not love him.[243]

45. Those to whom the word was spoken were of the nature of the Devil.[244] (See Fragment 44.)

46. [John 8:44] The Devil does not have will, but desires. . . . These things were spoken not to the natural earthbound sons of the Devil but to the animate beings (*psychikoi*), who by choice become sons of the Devil; from being such by nature, some can also by choice become sons of God. By having loved the desires of the Devil and doing them, these become children of the Devil, though they were not such by nature. In three ways one must bear the name "children": first by nature, second by inclination, third by merit. By nature is that which is born from some parent, which is

properly called "child"; by inclination, when someone does someone else's will through his own inclination; by merit, in the way some are called "children of Gehenna" [Matt. 23:15] and "darkness" and "lawlessness" and "offspring of snakes and vipers" [3:7; 12:34; 23:33]; for these do not beget any offspring according to their own nature, for they are ruinous and wasteful of those who are dashed against them; but since they performed their works they are called their children. . . . He now calls them "children of the Devil," not that the Devil begets any offspring, but that by doing the works of the Devil they became like him.[245]

47. [John 8:44] For his nature is not of truth but of the opposite of truth—deceit and ignorance. Therefore he can neither stand in the truth nor have truth in him, since he has falsehood in his own nature, and by nature is never able to speak the truth. Not only is he a liar, but so is his father . . . who receives his nature, since he arises from deceit and falsehood.[246]

48. [John 8:50: "I do not seek my glory; there is one who seeks and judges."] The "one who seeks and judges" is the one who avenges me, the servant commisioned for this, the one "not bearing the sword in vain," the "avenger" of the king [Rom. 13:4]. This is Moses as he prophesied to them, saying, "On whom you hoped" [John 5:45]. The one who "judges" and punishes is Moses, who himself is the lawgiver. How then does he say that "all judgment" was given to him [5:27]? He speaks rightly, for the judge doing his will judges as an avenger, just as also it appears to be done among men.[247]

Fragments on Matthew from Clement

49. [Matt. 3:11: John said, "I baptize you with water, but after me there comes he who will baptize you in spirit and fire."] He baptized no one in fire; but some, as Heracleon says, understand by "fire" the ears of those who are baptized, interpreting the Apostle's word in this way.[248]

50. [Matt. 10:32–33: "Everyone who will confess in[249] me before men, I will confess in him before my Father in heaven; whoever will deny me before men, I will deny him before my Father in heaven."] There is one confession which is made by faith and conduct and another made by voice. The confession by voice made before the authorities is what the many suppose is the only confession. They are wrong, for hypocrites can also make this confession. Their opinion will not be found confirmed universally, for not all the saved confessed by their voice and departed; of these are Matthew, Philip, Thomas, Levi, and many others. Confession by the voice is not universal but is for a few. But that which he now mentions [Matt.

10:32] is universal, by deeds and actions corresponding to faith in him. This confession is followed by that which is for a few, that before the authorities if it is necessary and reason requires it. For he will confess with his voice who has rightly first confessed with his character. And he has well used the expression "in me" of those who confess; [simply] "me" of those who deny. For the latter, though they confess him with the voice, deny him since they do not confess him in their conduct. The only ones who confess "in him" are those who live by their confession and conduct according to him, and he also confesses "in them," contained in them and held by them. Therefore he "never can deny himself" [2 Tim. 2:13]; but those who are not in him deny him. For he did not say, "Whoever shall deny in me" but ["Whoever shall deny"] "me." For no one who is in him will ever deny him. The expression "before men" applies both to the saved and likewise to the heathen; by conduct before the former and by voice before the latter.[250]

37
APELLES

It is not certain that Apelles, the famous early exegete of Genesis, was a follower of Marcion when he wrote his *Syllogisms*. The purely critical notions Apelles set forth owe nothing to Marcionite teaching and follow the lines of ancient rational exegesis. We cannot say, however, that Apelles always relied exclusively on such considerations. A certain Rhodo, perhaps teaching at Rome, debated with Apelles when he was an old man and noted that he took refuge in an appeal to faith after being "convicted of making many false statements." He "used to say that it is not necessary to investigate (*exetazein*) the matter fully, but each should remain in his own belief. Those who placed their hope on the Crucified would be saved, provided that they continued in good works." When asked for proof of the divine unity, he again appealed to faith but refused to use the Old Testament prophecies, which he considered "inconsistent (*asymphônoi*) and false and self-contradictory." After he made such an appeal, Rhodo ridiculed him for not knowing how to demonstrate what he taught.[251]

Almost all the exegetical fragments of Apelles come from Ambrose's *On Paradise* and, behind it, probably from Tertullian's treatise *Against the Followers of Apelles*.[252] The fragment on Noah's Ark quoted by Origen does not come via Tertullian, however.

The Inadequate Size of Noah's Ark

1. In no way could it have been accomplished that in so short a time so many kinds of animals and their foods, which were to last for a whole year, should be taken aboard. For when two by two the unclean animals, that is, two male and two female of each—this is what the repeated word means—and seven by seven the clean animals, that is, seven pairs, are described as led into the ark, how could the space described be made big enough to take even four elephants alone? It is clear that the story is false; but if this is so, it is clear that this writing is not from God.[253]

Adam and the Trees in Eden

2. (a) How does the tree of life seem to effect more for life than the breath of God? If God did not make man perfect, but each one through his own industry attains perfection of virtue for himself, does not man seem to acquire more for himself than God gave him? And if man had not tasted death, he did not know what he had not tasted. Therefore if he had not tasted, he was ignorant; if he was ignorant, he could not fear. Therefore vainly God presented death as a terror, since man did not fear it.[254]

(b) It is not always evil not to obey a precept. For if the precept is good, the obedience is honorable, but if the precept is wicked, it is proper to disobey. Therefore it is not always evil not to obey a precept, but it is wrong not to obey a good precept. Yet the tree of the knowledge of good and evil is a good work of the Demiurge, since God knows good and evil. Therefore he says, Behold, Adam has become like one of us. If then it is good to have the knowledge of good and evil, and the knowledge which God has is good, he who refuses it to men does not seem to refuse rightly.[255]

(c) He who does not know good and evil is no different from a child; and before a just judge a child is not guilty. A just Demiurge would never have accused a child of crime because of his not knowing good and evil, for a child has no guilt for transgression and crime.[256]

(d) He who does not know good and evil did not even know himself to be evil in not keeping the commandment, nor did he know it to be good [not] to obey evil. Therefore he who did not obey was worthy of pardon, not condemnation.[257]

(e) Whence did death come to Adam, from the nature of a tree of this sort or indeed from God? If we ascribe it to the nature of the tree, the fruit of this tree seems to surpass the life-giving breath of God [see 2a], if indeed the person whom the breath made alive was brought to death by the fruit of this tree. Or if we say that God is the agent of death, we accuse him on a double charge: either he is so harsh that he would not forgive when he could, or so weak, if he could not forgive.[258]

God's Foreknowledge and Adam's Sin

3. (a) Did God know Adam would transgress his commandments or did he not? If he did not know, there is no declaration of the divine power; if however he knew and nevertheless gave orders that had to be neglected, it is not godlike to give a superfluous command; yet he gave a superfluous command to that first-formed Adam, which he knew he would not keep at all; yet God does nothing superfluous; therefore the writing is not of God.[259]

(b) Did he who created man and engraved on him these beliefs about good and evil know that man would sin, or did he not? For there is no human creature made by God which was not commanded by God. Therefore the creation of man is not of God, because God does not make evil; but man accepted the belief about evil when he was told to keep away from evil.[260]

The Question of God's Goodness

4. (a) How is God good when he not only suffered evil to come into this world but allowed it to come into such confusion?[261]

(b) There is one good God and a single first principle and a single nameless power; the one God and the single principle have no concern for the things which happen here in this world. But that same holy and good God from above made another god, and the other god created everything, heaven and earth and everything in the world. But he was not all good, and the things made by him were not made well; but everything was created by him in accordance with his evil intelligence.[262]

The Serpent with Eve in Eden

5. How can the serpent, by nature irrational and created mute by God, speak rationally and vocally? For if of itself it had the power to reason and judge and understand and reply to the words spoken by the woman, nothing would keep any serpent from doing this. But if they say it addressed Eve with a human voice in accordance with God's will and dispensation, they make God the cause of sin.

It was impossible for the evil demon to grant a voice to one naturally mute so that it could be what it was not before; otherwise he would not have stopped conversing with men and leading them astray through serpents and wild animals and birds.

And how did an animal hear the commandment which was given secretly by God only to man, without even the woman learning of it? Why did he not attack the man rather than the woman? And if you say he assaulted the weaker one [I reply that] on the contrary, she was the stronger, the helper of man, as she was shown to be in the transgression of the commandment. For she alone resists the serpent, and only after she was defeated by revolt and craft did she eat of the tree. But Adam did not wholly struggle or reply, but took the fruit given by the woman, demonstrating the greatest weakness and an unmanly mind. The woman, overcome by the demon, deserves pardon, but Adam, as one overcome by a woman, does not; he himself had received the commandment from God. But the woman, hearing the commandment from Adam, despised it, or thought it unworthy of God to speak it, or doubted it, thinking that Adam had taken it on himself to give the commandment to her.

When she was by herself, the serpent found her, so it could speak privately to her. Seeing her eating the fruits of trees, it mentioned the fruit of the tree of knowledge, which was not eaten. And if eaten, obviously it would have been in a corruptible body, for "everything that goes into the mouth passes into the drain" [Matt. 15:17]. So if corruptible, then evidently also mortal. And if mortal, this was no longer a curse, nor was that word spoken to man by the voice of God: "You are earth, and to earth you will return" [Gen. 3:19], at least according to the truth of the matter.

Again, if the serpent did not see the woman eating, how did it induce her to eat when she had never eaten before? And who showed this murderous and criminal serpent that the word of God would have no easement, the word about death which said, "The day when you eat, you shall surely die" [Gen. 2:17]? Not only that, but that with this perception their eyes were opened, which did not see before? By this so-called "opening" they approached death.[263]

38
GAIUS ON NEW TESTAMENT BOOKS

Eusebius quotes fragments of Gaius of Rome (end of the second century) on Christian antiquities but not his criticisms of the Gospel and

Apocalypse of John, for which we have to rely on the account of the "Alogi" by Epiphanius and on the twelfth-century commentary by Dionysius Bar Salibi.

Dialogue with [the Montanist] *Proclus* (Fragments 1–4)

1. But I can point out the trophies of the apostles. For if you are willing to go to the Vatican or to the Via Ostia, you will find the trophies of those who founded the church.[264]

For the discovery of a "trophy" under St. Peter's see J. Toynbee and J. Ward Perkins, *The Shrine of St. Peter and the Vatican Excavations* (New York: Pantheon, 1957).

2. But Cerinthus too, by means of revelations supposed to be written by a great apostle [John], falsely introduces wonderful stories to us as if they had been shown him by angels. He says that after the resurrection Christ's kingdom will be on earth, and the flesh, dwelling at Jerusalem, will again serve lusts and pleasures. And being an enemy to God's scriptures and wishing to deceive, he says there will be a period of a thousand years for wedding festivities.[265]

3. Proclus speaks thus: "But after him there were four prophetesses, daughters of Philip, at Hierapolis in Asia. Their tomb is there, and that of their father."[266]

4. While curbing the recklessness and audacity of his opponents in composing new scriptures, he mentions only thirteen epistles of the holy apostle, not counting the Epistle to the Hebrews with the rest; as even to this day there are some among the Romans who do not consider it to be the apostle's.[267]

The "Alogi" of Epiphanius (Fragments 5–13)

5. They say that these books are not by John but by Cerinthus, and are not worthy to exist in the church.[268]

6. They say that his [John's] books do not agree with the other apostles. "What does it say? 'In the beginning was the Logos and the Logos was with God and the Logos was God, and the Logos became flesh and tabernacled among us and we beheld his glory, glory as of the Only-begotten of the Father, full of grace and truth' [John 1:1–2, 14], and immediately following, 'John bore witness and cried, saying, "This is he of whom I spoke to you"' [1:15] and, 'This is the Lamb of God, who takes away the

sin of the world' [1:29]; and after that it says, 'And they who heard said to him, Rabbi, where do you dwell?' [1:38]. And in the same place, 'The next day Jesus wanted to go to Galilee, and he finds Philip and says to him, Follow me' [1:43]. And a little beyond this, 'And after three days there was a wedding in Cana of Galilee, and Jesus was invited to the wedding, and his disciples with him, and his mother was there' [2:1–2]. But the other evangelists say he spent forty days in the desert, tempted by the Devil, and then returned and took the disciples to himself."[269]

7. See how the second Gospel makes it clear concerning Christ [Mark 1:1] but nowhere mentions being born again [John 3:3]; but it says, "In the Jordan the Spirit came upon him, and a voice, 'This is the beloved Son, in whom I am well pleased'" [Matt. 3:16–17].[270]

8. How did the other evangelists say that Jesus took flight from the presence of Herod into Egypt, and after the flight came and remained at Nazareth; then receiving baptism he went away into the desert, and after that returned, and after his return began to preach?[271]

9. "John spoke of the Savior's keeping two Passovers [2:13; 6:4; 13:1], but the other evangelists, only one."[272]

10. We find expressed somewhere in these writings the notion that the divine Logos was begotten of God in the fortieth [*mu*] year of Augustus. Either the writer made a mistake or because the *beta* dropped out and only the *mu* remained he wrote only forty years. For he was begotten in the forty-second [*mu beta*] year of Augustus. He also says it was on the twelfth day before the Kalends of July or June, I do not remember which, in the consulship of Sulpicius Camerinus[273] and Vettius Pompeianus. I noticed this because those who mention the day of the conception, when Gabriel told the news to the Virgin, share the opinion of some who say that according to tradition he was born in seven months.[274]

11. Of what value to me is the Apocalypse of John, which tells about seven angels and seven trumpets [Rev. 8:2]?[275]

12. Again, it says, "Write to the angel of the church in Thyatira" [Rev. 2:18], but no church existed at Thyatira. How then did he write to a nonexistent church?[276]

13. These incompetent word-chasers reject the Gospel and Apocalypse of John, and even his epistles, which agree with the Gospel and Apocalypse. And they say, "I saw, and he said to the angel, 'Loose the four angels which are in the Euphrates.' And I heard the number of the army, ten thousand times ten thousand, and a thousand times a thousand, and they were clad in breastplates of fire and brimstone and hyacinth" [Rev. 9:14–17]. They think the truth is "ridiculous."[277]

From Dionysius bar Salibi (Fragments 14–17)

14. Hippolytus of Rome said, "There was a man named Gaius who claimed that neither the Gospel nor the Apocalypse was John's but belonged to the heretic Cerinthus."[278]

15. The heretic Gaius charged John with disagreeing with his fellow-evangelists since he says that after the baptism he went into Galilee and wrought the miracle of the wine at Cana.[279]

16. (a) It is impossible that these things [described in Rev. 8:12] should take place, for "the coming of the Lord will take place like a thief in the night" [1 Thess. 5:2].

(b) As in the flood the heavenly bodies were not taken away [against Rev. 8:12], so it will happen at the End, according to the Scripture [cf. Matt. 24:37] and the writing of Paul; "when they say Peace and security, then their destruction will be at hand" [1 Thess. 5:3].

(c) How can the lawless be tormented by locusts [Rev. 9:3–5] when the Scripture says that sinners prosper and the righteous are persecuted in the world [Ps. 73:2, Job 21:9], and Paul says that believers shall be persecuted and evil men shall grow worse, deceiving and deceived [2 Tim. 3:12–13]?

(d) It is not written that angels shall war nor that a quarter of mankind shall be destroyed [Rev. 9:14–15 (a third)], but that "Nation shall rise against nation" [Matt. 24:7].[280]

17. "How can Satan be bound here [Rev. 20:2] when it is written that Christ entered into the house of the strong man and bound him and took his goods away from him" [Matt. 12:29]?[281]

39
PSEUDO-TERTULLIAN AGAINST ALL HERESIES

This little treatise was once identified as the work to which Justin referred in *Apology* 1.26 (see chap. 30), but it is certainly later than Irenaeus. It gives a succinct account of the leading second-century heresies. The text is from CC 1, 1401–10.

1.1. About these heretics, to pass over most items, I shall state a few things. I do not mention the heretics of Judaism; I mean Dositheus the Samaritan, who first ventured to reject the prophets as not having spoken in the Holy Spirit, and the Sadducees, who rising up from the root of his error to this heresy have ventured to deny the resurrection of the flesh. I omit the

Pharisees, who are separated from the Jews by their addition of certain items to the Law, from which addition they were made worthy to receive the name that they bear, and with these the Herodians, who say that Herod was the Christ. I turn to those who chose to be heretics from the Gospel.

1.2. Of these the first of all is Simon Magus, who in the Acts of the Apostles deserved his fitting and just sentence from the apostle Peter. He ventured to say that he was the highest power, that is, the highest God, and that the world was created by his angels, and that he had come down into a wandering demon, which was Wisdom, and that he did not suffer among the Jews in the form of God but seemed to suffer. 1.3. After him his disciple Menander, also a magician, taught the same doctrines as Simon and styled himself whatever Simon had called himself. He denied that anyone could obtain salvation unless he had been baptized in his name. 1.4. After these there followed Saturninus, and he similarly said that the unbegotten power, that is, God, remains in the highest and infinite regions above. Far distant from this the angels made a lower world, and because a certain effulgence of light had shone down into the lower regions, the angels took charge of creating man in the likeness of that light. Man lay creeping on the earth, but that light and that higher power mercifully saved his soul by a spark. The rest of man perishes. Christ did not exist in a substantial body; he suffered as a phantom. There is certainly no resurrection of the flesh.

1.5. Later the heretic Basilides burst forth. He says the highest God is named Abraxas, the name by which he calls the created Mind (in Greek, *nous*). Thence came the Word; from it Providence, Power, and Wisdom; from them were made principalities, powers, and angels; thence infinite emissions and emanations of angels; by those angels the 365 heavens were created, as well as the world, in honor of Abraxas, whose name has this number computed in it.[282] He places the most recent of all the angels, the god of the Jews, among the last angels and those who made this world. This was the god of the Law and the prophets, whom he denies to be a god but calls an angel. The seed of Abraham fell to him by lot and therefore he brought the sons of Israel out of the land of Egypt into the land of Canaan. He was more turbulent than the other angels and therefore frequently stirred up seditions and wars and poured out human blood. But Christ, sent not by this one but by Abraxas, came as a phantom without the substance of flesh. He did not suffer among the Jews but Simon was crucified in his place.[283] Therefore none ought to believe in him "who was crucified," lest he confess his belief in Simon. He says martyrdoms should not be performed. He sharply opposes the resurrection of the flesh and denies that salvation was promised to bodies.

1.6. Another heretic, Nicolaus, emerged. He was one of the seven deacons who were chosen in the Acts of the Apostles [6:5]. He says darkness was desired by the light, as well as shameful and obscene things; from this mixture came nasty and impure things it is shameful to mention. There are also other obscene matters. He mentions certain aeons, born of evil and embraces and damnable mixtures and mingled obscenities and certain things even wickeder than these. Afterwards demons and gods and seven spirits were born, and other things, sacrilegious and obscene, which we should blush to tell and therefore omit. It is enough for us that the whole heresy of the Nicolaitans was condemned by the Apocalypse of the Lord, by the very weighty authority of the sentence which says, "Because you have this, you hate the teaching of the Nicolaitans, which I hate too" [Rev. 2:6].[284]

2.1. To these there succeeded the heretics who are called Ophites. For they exalt the snake [*ophis*] so much that they even prefer it to Christ. For they say it gave us the knowledge of good and evil. Noticing its power and majesty, Moses made a snake of brass and those who looked on it received their health. Christ himself, they also say, in his gospel imitates the holy power of the snake when he says, "And as Moses lifted up the snake in the wilderness, even so the Son of Man must be lifted up" [John 3:14]. They bring it in to bless their eucharist. 2.2. But the whole occasion and teaching of that error flows from this: they say that from the highest and primal Aeon many other lower Aeons have come into existence, but that Aeon whose name is Ialdabaoth is superior to all these. He was conceived from the other Aeon by mingling with lower Aeons and afterward, when he wanted to go up into the region above, the weight of the matter mixed in him kept him from reaching the higher place but, left in between, he spread out completely and thus made the heaven. 2.3. Ialdabaoth, however, went down lower and made seven sons for himself; he stopped the upper regions from spreading, so that since the angels could not know what was above they might consider him the only god. Therefore those powers and lower angels made man, and he lay creeping like a worm because he was created by the weaker, mediocre powers. But that Aeon from whom Ialdabaoth proceeded, moved by envy, sent down a certain spark into man as he lay, by which he might be aroused and grow wise through prudence and be able to understand things above. 2.4. Thus again Ialdabaoth becoming indignant gave out from himself the power and likeness of the snake, and this was the power in paradise. In other words, that was the snake in which Eve believed as if he were the Son of God. She took of the fruit of the tree, they say, and therefore gave the knowledge of good and evil to mankind. Christ was not in the substance of flesh. Salvation for the flesh is not to be hoped for.

2.5. Then there burst forth another heresy, called that of the Cainites. For they exalt Cain as if he had been conceived from a certain mighty power which worked in him. For Abel was created, conceived from a lower power and therefore found inferior. Those who assert this even defend the traitor Judas, calling him admirable and great because of the useful services he is boasted to have brought to mankind. 2.6. Some of them think thanks should be given Judas for this reason: Judas, they say, thinking that Christ was going to overthrow the truth, betrayed him so that the truth might not be overthrown. And others dispute from the other side and say this: because the powers of this world did not want Christ to suffer, lest salvation be prepared for mankind through his death, [Judas] planning for the salvation of mankind, betrayed Christ so that salvation, which was being obstructed by the powers who stood in the way to keep Christ from suffering, could not be impeded and therefore by the passion of Christ the salvation of mankind could not be delayed.

2.7. But that heresy also came forth which is called that of the Sethians. The doctrine of this perversity is as follows. Two men were created by the angels: Cain and Abel. On this account that power above all powers, which they call Mother, desired this Seth to be conceived and born in Abel's place, so that those angels who had created the two men might become ineffectual, since this seed, the world, arises and is born. 2.8. For they say that there were wicked minglings of angels and men, and therefore that power, which as we said they call Mother, brought about the flood for punishment, so that that seed of mingling might be taken away and only this seed which was pure might be kept intact. 2.9. But they who created beings from the earlier seed secretly and surreptitiously, without the knowledge of that power which they call Mother, sent the seed of Ham with those eight souls in the ark, so that the seed of malice might not perish but be preserved with the rest and after the flood return to earth and grow, as an example to the others, and spread out and fill and occupy the whole earth. They think that Christ was only Seth and Seth himself was in his place.

3.1. Afterwards Carpocrates introduced this sect: he says there is one power, chief among those above, from which the angels and powers were produced; and they, far removed from the upper powers, created the world in the lower regions. Christ was not born of the virgin Mary but begotten as a mere man from the seed of Joseph. Of course he was outstanding in his pursuit of virtue and integrity of life. Only his soul was received into heaven, because it was firmer and stronger than others. From this he deduces that only the salvation of souls is to be maintained; there are no resurrections of the body.

3.2. After him burst forth the heretic Cerinthus, who taught similar doctrines. For he also says the world was created by them; he states that Christ was born of the seed of Joseph, arguing that he was only a man without any divinity, and holding that the Law also was given by the angels. The god of the Jews is not Lord, but an angel.

3.3. His successor was Ebion, who did not agree with Cerinthus in every respect, for he said that the world was made by God, not by the angels. And because it is written, "No disciple is greater than his master, nor a slave than his lord" [Matt. 10:24], he upheld the Law, no doubt in order to exclude the Gospel and vindicate Judaism.

4.1. The heretic Valentinus introduced many myths. I will condense them and briefly set them forth. He brings in the Pleroma and thirty Aeons and he explains them through *syzygies* [pairs]. For he says that in the beginning were Depth and Silence; from these came Mind and Truth, from which burst forth Word and Life, from which again were created Man and Church. Now from these there also proceeded twelve Aeons, and from Word and Life ten others. This is the thirty-fold Aeon, which is made up in the Pleroma of the Eight, the Ten, and the Twelve. 4.2. The thirtieth Aeon wanted to see Depth and to see him ventured into the upper regions. Because it was not capable of the greatness of seeing him, it was in revolt and would have been dissolved unless the one sent to make it firm, named Limit, had settled it by saying "Iao." 4.3. That Aeon made for revolt he calls Achamoth and says that it felt certain passions of desire and from the passions brought forth matter. For it was frightened, he says, and afraid and sad; and from these passions it conceived and brought forth. [Hence it made heaven and earth and sea and everything in them.][285] 4.4. Therefore everything is weak and fragile and perishable and mortal, everything made by it, because it was itself conceived and brought forth from revolt. Yet it created the world from those materials which Achamoth supplied by dreading or fearing or mourning or sweating. For from dread, he says, darkness was made; from fear and ignorance, the spirit of wrongdoing and wickedness; from sadness and tears, the wet materials of springs, rivers, and the sea. 4.5. Christ was sent by the forefather Depth, but he was in the substance not of our body but of some sort of spiritual body coming down from heaven. He passed through the virgin Mary like water through a pipe, receiving nothing from her and not being changed. He denies the resurrection of this flesh. 4.6. He approves of some things in the Law and the prophets and disapproves of some; or rather, he disapproves of all and rejects some. He has his own Gospel instead of those we have.

4.7. After him there arose the heretics Ptolemaeus and Secundus, who agree with Valentinus on almost everything and differ only on this point. For while Valentinus fixed the number of Aeons at thirty, they have added several others; they have collected four at the beginning, then another four. And they deny what Valentinus stated, that the thirtieth Aeon left the Pleroma as in revolt; for the one in revolt because of its desire to see the forefather did not belong to that thirtyfold group.

4.8. Then arose another heretic, Heracleon, who agreed with Valentinus but by a certain novelty of expression wants to seem to have different thoughts. For he holds that in the beginning was that which he calls Lord, then from that [monad] proceeded two, then the rest of the Aeons. Then he brings in all of Valentinus.

5.1. After these there did not fail to arise a certain Marcus and Color-basus, who composed a new heresy from the Greek alphabet. They deny that truth can be reached without those letters; indeed, they hold that the whole fullness and perfection of truth lies in those letters. For this reason Christ said, "I am Alpha and Omega" [Rev. 1:8, etc.]. 5.2. When Jesus Christ came down, really a dove descended on Jesus; since its Greek name is *peristera,* it has in it the number 801.[286] They mention *omega, psi, chi, phi, upsilon, tau*[287]—in fact everything, even *alpha* and *beta,* and figure out ogdoads and decads. To discuss all their vanities would be stupid and tiresome. 5.3. But what is not so vain, but dangerous instead, is that they imagine another god beside the Creator and deny that Christ was in the substance of flesh; they deny the future resurrection of the body.

6.1. A certain Cerdo came next. He introduces two beginnings, that is, two gods, one good and the other cruel; the good one, higher, the cruel one, creator of this world. He rejects prophecies and the Law, he renounces the creator god, and he holds that Christ came as the son of the higher god. He denies that he was in the substance of flesh and says he existed only as a phantom; he did not suffer at all, but seemed to suffer; nor was he born of a virgin—he was not born at all. He approves only of the resurrection of the soul and denies that of the body. He accepts only the Gospel of Luke and not all of that. He does not use all the epistles of the apostle Paul, nor does he use them complete. He rejects the Acts of the Apostles and the Apocalypse as false.

6.2. After him arose his disciple, Marcion by name, from Pontus, the son of a bishop, who was expelled from the communion of the church because of the seduction of a certain virgin. Since it was said, "Every good tree bears good fruit, and an evil tree evil" [Matt. 7:17], he ventured to assent to the heresy of Cerdo and to say the same things that the earlier heretic had said before.

6.3. There arose after him a certain Lucan, follower and disciple of Marcion. Going through the same kinds of blasphemy, he taught the same things that Marcion and Cerdo had taught.

6.4. After these there followed Ap[p]elles, a disciple of Marcion, who after falling in regard to the flesh was removed by Marcion. He introduces one god in the infinite upper regions. He made many powers as well as the angels and, in addition, another power which he says is called Lord but is really an angel. He wants the world considered as the creation of this [Lord] in imitation of the world above. He was filled with regret over the world because he did not make it as perfectly as that world above had been made. He rejects the Law and the prophets. 6.5. He says that Christ was neither a phantom, as Marcion teaches, nor a being in the substance of a true body, as the Gospel teaches; but because he came down from the regions above, in his descent he wove for himself a flesh of stars and air. Ascending in the resurrection, he gave back to the various elements what had been changed in his descending, and thus when the various parts of his body were dispersed he gave back only his spirit into heaven [cf. Luke 23:46]. 6.6. He denies the resurrection of the flesh. He uses the Apostle, but in Marcion's incomplete collection. He says that salvation is only for souls. In addition he has private and extraordinary texts of his own, which he calls the *Visions* of a girl named Philumene ["beloved"], whom he follows as a prophetess. He also has his own books of *Syllogisms*, which he wrote, in which he tries to prove that everything Moses wrote about God is not true but false.

7.1. To all these heretics there succeeded another, Tatian. He was a disciple of Justin Martyr, after whose death he became unorthodox. For he understands things entirely in accord with Valentinus, adding only this, that Adam cannot be saved, as if when the branches are saved the root is not saved too.

7.2. There arose other heretics who are called Cataphrygians, but their doctrine is not uniform. For there are those called Kata ["according to"] Proclus and others, according to Aeschines. These have one blasphemy in common and another not in common but peculiar to themselves. The common one is that they say the Holy Spirit was in the apostles, but not the Paraclete; the Paraclete said more things to Montanus than Christ set forth in the gospel—not only more, but better and greater. Those who are Kata Aeschines have this to add: they say Christ himself was Son and Father.

8.1. After all these came Blastus, who secretly tried to introduce Judaism. For he says the Pascha must be kept only according to the Law of Moses, on the fourteenth of the month. Who does not know that God's grace is made void if you reduce Christ to the Law?

8.2. Theodotus the heretic from Byzantium followed these; after he was arrested for the name of Christ and denied, he did not stop blaspheming Christ, for he introduced the teaching which called Christ just a man and denied he was God. Though he was born of the Holy Spirit and the Virgin, he was a mere man, superior to others only by the significance of his righteousness. 8.3. Another heretic Theodotus arose after him; he too introduced another sect and said that Christ was only a man, conceived and born of the Holy Spirit and the Virgin. But he was inferior to Melchizedek, because it was said of Christ, "You are a priest for ever, after the order of Melchizedek" [Heb. 5:6, etc.]. For that Melchizedek is a heavenly power of special grace, because what Christ does for men by becoming their intercessor and advocate, Melchizedek does for the heavenly angels and powers. For he is better than Christ, since he is fatherless, motherless, without genealogy, and his beginning and end is neither comprehended nor comprehensible.

8.4. But after all these, Praxeas also introduced a heresy, which Victorinus[288] also took care to strengthen. He says that God the Father Almighty is Jesus Christ; he argues that he was crucified, he suffered, he died; and with profane and sacrilegious boldness he states that afterwards he sat down at his own right hand.

Abbreviations

CCL   Corpus Christianorum, Series latina
NAPS   North American Patristic Society
ILS   *Inscriptiones latinae selectae* (Dessau)
LCL   Loeb Classical Library
PG   Patrologia graeca
PL   Patrologia latina
SC   Sources chrétiennes

Notes

1. Arrian, *Discourses of Epictetus* 4.7.6.

2. See R. L. Wilken, *The Christians as the Romans Saw Them* (New Haven, Conn.: Yale University Press, 1984), 1–30.

3. For twenty years as a long time in court cases (Pliny, *Epistles* 10.110–11).

4. Pliny, *Epistles* 10.97. The precedent in question was set in the reign of Domitian (Pliny, *Panegyric* 34–36; Suetonius, *Domitian* 12.1). In *Epistle* 55 Trajan speaks of "the justice of our times."

5. Tacitus, *Histories* 5.9.

6. Fire: Tacitus, *Annals* 15.38–43.

7. Christians: Tacitus, *Annals* 15.44.

8. Suetonius, *Claudius* 25.4.

9. *Nero* 16.2. "Superstition" again, as in Pliny and Tacitus.

10. Justin, *Apology* 1.68; Eusebius, *Church History* 4.9.

11. Minucius Felix, *Octavius* 9.8 (31.1).

12. C. R. Haines, *The Correspondence of Marcus Cornelius Fronto* 2 (LCL, 1930), 284 n.1.

13. Marcus Aurelius, *Meditations* 11.3 (*atragôdôs*). Oddly, Marcus goes on to praise tragedy in 11.6.

14. Lucian, *Alexander* 25.

15. Ibid., 38.

16. Lucian, *Peregrinus* 11–13.

17. Ibid., 16.

18. Generally, Wilken, *The Christians*, 68–93.

19. R. Walzer, *Galen on Jews and Christians* (London: Oxford University Press, 1949); Marcus Aurelius, *Meditations* 11.3; Hippolytus, *Refutation* 9.12.10–11.

20. Galen, *Antidotes*, 14.65 Kühn; Tertullian, *To Scapula* 4.5–6.

21. *On the Differences of Pulses* (8.579 and 657 Kühn); *On the First Unmoved Mover* (Arabic); Walzer, *Galen*, 13–15.

22. *Summary of Plato's Republic* (Arabic); Walzer, *Galen*, 15–16.

23. Walzer, *Galen on Jews* 67 = Galen, *On Moral Conduct*, 14 Kraus. "We have actually seen in our own time slaves who acted thus, quite differently from freeborn people, because they were free by nature; for when [the praetorian prefect] Perennis died—and his death took place in the ninth year of Commodus, under the consulship of Maternus and Bradua [185]— many people were persecuted and their slaves were tortured to reveal the activities of their masters. This indicates that the love of the noble exists in some people by nature, even when they have not been educated." (The "ninth year" is counted from 176.)

24. Galen, *On the Passions of the Soul*, 5.30 Kühn = *Scripta minora* 1.23, 11–16 Marquardt.

25. H. Chadwick, *The Sentences of Sextus* (Cambridge: Cambridge University Press, 1959).

26. Walzer, *Galen,* 11; *On His Own Books* 1 (19.13–14 Kühn) (between 162 and 166).

27. Walzer, *Galen,* 12–13; *On the Use of the Parts of the Body* 11.14, 2.158 Helmrich (between 169 and 176).

28. Walzer, *Galen,* 14; *On the Differences of Pulses* 3.3 (8.657 Kühn) (176–180).

29. Walzer, *Galen,* 14; *On the Differences of Pulses* 2.4 (8.579 Kühn).

30. Walzer, *Galen,* 13–15 (from Arabic of *On the Prime Unmoved Mover*).

31. Walzer, *Galen,* 15–16 (Arabic excerpt from Galen's lost summary of Plato's *Republic*) (about 180).

32. Based on something like the beatitudes in *Acts of Paul and Thecla* 5, 238–39 Lipsius.

33. Perhaps the first (derogatory) instance of *prosértémena* (or *prosartéma*) occurs in Galen, *Doctrines of Hippocrates and Plato* 4.5 (5.396 Kühn), possibly echoing Posidonius; next comes Epictetus 1.9.11, cited by A. S. L. Farquharson (*The Meditations of the Emperor Marcus Antoninus* [Oxford: Clarendon Press, 1944], 885), followed by Marcus Aurelius himself (*Meditations* 12.3). From this Stoic setting the term passes into Christian Gnostic usage by Isidore, son of the Gnostic Basilides (Clement, *Miscellanies* 2.113.3–114.1), by other (?) Basilidians (ibid., 112.1–2), and by Julius Cassianus as cited here.

34. Clement, *Miscellanies* 3.91–92.

35. Also Epiphanius, *Heresies* 26.3.1. "I stood on a high mountain and I saw a tall man and another short one and I heard something like the sound of thunder and I drew near to hear it and it spoke to me and said, 'I am you and you are I and wherever you are I am there and I am scattered in all and wherever you may wish to collect me, by collecting me you collect yourself.'"

36. Origen in Eusebius, *Church History* 6.19.12–13.

37. Clement, *Prophetic Selections* 55.

38. Maximus, *Scholia on Gregory of Nazianzus* (PG 91.1085AB).

39. Origen, *Against Celsus* 4.52.

40. Jerome, *Commentary on Galatians* 2.3.13 (PL 26.387B).

41. Jerome, *Hebrew Questions on Genesis* 2 (CCL 72.3). Presumably based on *be-reshith* (Gen. 1:1); *reshith = arché*.

42. Maximus, *Scholia on Dionysius Mystical Theology* 1 (PG 4.421BC). Seven heavens in Christian and Gnostic speculation: H. Crouzel and M. Simonetti, *Origène Traité des principes* 2 (Paris: Cerf, 1978), 151–52.

43. Eusebius, *Church History* 4.6.3.

44. Ibid., 4.22.8.

45. Ibid., 4.22.7.

46. C. C. Torrey, "James the Just and his Name 'Oblias,'" *Journal of Biblical Literature* 63 (1944): 93–98; emends Oblias to Obdias (Obadiah). Philip Carrington noted that Hegesippus's original if Hebrew must have ended =*am* (= "people").

47. *thura*; perhaps emend to *torah*? But the *Second Apocalypse of James*, 55.7, refers to the "good door"; A. Böhlig and P. Labib, *Koptisch-Gnostische Apokalypsen aus Codex V von Nag Hammadi* (Halle-Wittenberg: Martin-Luther Universität, 1963), 77.

48. Cf. John 19:38–39.

49. Cf. James 2:1–10.

50. See note 47.

51. Eusebius, *Church History* 2.23.4–18. Vespasian attacked about eight years after James was killed.

52. Ibid., 4.22.4.

53. Ibid., 3.32.3.

54. Ibid., 3.32.6.

55. Ibid., 3.32.7–8.

56. Ibid., 3.20.1.

57. Ibid., 4.8.2.

58. Presumably a list of names.

59. Ibid., 4.22.2–3.

60. Stephanus Gobarus in Photius, *Library* 232 (PG 103.1096AB).

61. Eusebius, *Church History* 5.19. See chap. 17, fragment 4.

62. Ibid., 6.12.3–6.

63. Ibid., 3.39.4. For fragments of Papias see chap. 16.

64. Maximus, *Scholia on Dionysius Ecclesiastical Hierarchies* 2 (PG 4.48D-49A).

65. Georgios Hamartolos, edited by H. Nolte, "Ein Excerpt aus dem grössten Theil noch ungedruckten Chronikon des Georgius Hamartolus." *Theologische Quartalschrift* 44 (1862): 464–68 (466); cf. Philip of Side, edited by C. de Boor, *Texte und Untersuchungen* 5.2 (1888), 170 (cf. 176–79).

66. Maximus, *Scholia on Dionysius Ecclesiastical Hierarchies* (PG 4.176C).

67. The total is thus 2.5 sextillion. Catullus (*Ode* 5) more moderately suggested setting the exaggerated numbers of his and Lesbia's kisses into confusion: *conturbabimus illa, ne sciamus, aut nequis malus invidere possit, cum tantum sciat esse basiorum.*

68. Irenaeus, *Heresies* 5.33.3–4; cf. Hippolytus, *Daniel* 4.60.

69. From Cramer's *Catena* on Acts 1:18 (*Catenae* 3.12); F. X. Funk and K. Bihlmeyer, *Die apostolischen Väter* (Tübingen: Mohr, 1956), 136–37; Schoedel, *Polycarp, Martyrdom of Polycarp, Fragments of Papias* (Camden, N.J.: Thomas Nelson & Sons, 1967), 111–12.

70. Eusebius, *Church History* 3.39.9–12.

71. Irenaeus, *Heresies* 5.36.1–2.

72. Andrew of Caesarea, *On the Apocalypse* 34.12 (PG 106.325CD).

73. Anastasius of Sinai, *Anagogical Contemplation on the Six Days' Work* 10 (PG 89.860BC, Latin); Greek in J. B. Pitra, *Analecta Sacra Spicilegio parata* II (Typis Tusculanis, 1884; repr. 1966), 160.

74. Eusebius, *Church History* 3.39.15.

75. Ibid., 3.39.16.

76. Apart from the other mixups, *exotericis* is presumably a garbled version of *exegeticis*.

77. Pitra, *Analecta Sacra*, 160.

78. On Apollinaris see R. M. Grant, *Greek Apologists of the Second Century* (Philadelphia: Westminster Press, 1988), 83–90.

79. Eusebius, *Church History* 4.27; 5.5.4.

80. Ibid., 5.5.3.

81. Themistius (*Oration* 15.276.19–29 Downey) refers to "the giver of life" and in 357 had seen a depiction of the event, perhaps on the column of Marcus Aurelius at Rome. *Scriptores Historiae Augustae M. Antoninus* 24.4 is not explicit: *fulmen de caelo precibus suis* (Marcus) *extorsit.*

82. Dio Cassius 71.8.4; Dio ascribes it to "the divine" (*to theion*, as in 60.9.4).

83. *Suidae Lexicon*, A 3987 (1.365 Adler).

84. Besieged by Quadi and Marcomanni in the time of Marcus Aurelius (Ammianus Marcellinus 29.6.1).

85. L'année épigraphique 1934, 245 = G. Brusin, *Gli scavi di Aquileia* (Udine: Edizioni de "La Panarie," 1934), 165–67. For Arnuphis's title cf. F. Cumont, *L'Égypte des astrologues* (Brussels: Fondation Reine Élisabeth, 1937), 121–22; also Clement of Alexandria *Miscellanies* 5.20.3 (they use hieratic); 6.36.1 (they know hieroglyphics, cosmography, geography, ritual); cf. Apuleius, *Metamorphoses* 11.17; Porphyry, *Abstinence* 4.8; Iamblichus, *Mysteries* 1.1. According to "the Egyptians" Osiris made Hermes his "sacred scribe" (Diodorus Siculus 1.16.2).

86. J. Guey, "Mage et dieu," Revue de philologie 22 (1948): 16–62. He compared the Ptolemaic inscription *Orientis Graeci Inscriptiones Selectae* 131, dedicated to "the greatest god Hermes, who is Paotpnouphis" (cf. 206, "to the greatest god Hermaos Pautnouphis") and *Papyri Graecae Magicae* 7.345 (*ANK SOS ERMAICHO*) and 558 (*THATH* and *SO*).

87. *Suidae Lexicon* 1:434 (2.642 Adler), with cross-reference to "Arnouphis"; cf. E. Boer in *Der Kleine Pauly* 2 (1967): 1519.

88. Earliest, Apollinaris in Eusebius *Church History* 5.5.4; cf. Tertullian, *Apology* 5.6; *To Scapula* 4.6.

89. Printed in LCL, *Dio's Roman History* 9.30–31.

90. This passage appears in the tenth-century *Suda* (A. S. L. Farquharson, *The Meditations of the Emperor Marcus Antoninus,* vol. 1:xviii, 4).

91. Dio Cassius 60.9.2–5. The term for "divine power" is *theion*, as in Dio's account of the other rain miracle.

92. *Paschal Chronicle*, preface (Corpus scriptorum historiae Byzantinae 16.13–14); O. Perler, *Méliton de Sardes Sur la Pâque et fragments* (SC 123; Paris: Cerf, 1966), 244–45.

93. Ibid., 16.14; Perler, *Méliton de Sardes*, 244–47.

94. Eusebius, *Church History* 5.19.2–4.

95. Jerome, *Illustrious Men* 24.

96. S. G. Hall, *Melito of Sardis On Pascha and Fragments* (Oxford: Clarendon Press, 1979), especially xxviii–xxxix.

97. Eusebius, *Church History* 4.26.5–11.

98. *Paschal Chronicle*, CSHB 16.483.

99. Eusebius, *Church History* 4.26.13–14.

100. See Hall, *Melito of Sardis*, xxi: L. Sergius Paulus consul 168? Q. Servilius Pudens, consul 166?

101. Eusebius, *Church History* 4.26.3–4.

102. Origen, *Selections on the Psalms* (PG 12.1120A).

103. J. B. Pitra, *Analecta Sacra* ii.3–5 (from Codex Vaticanus 2022, folios 238–39).

104. See R. M. Grant, "The Structure of Eucharistic Prayers," *Antiquity and Humanity: Essays on Ancient Religion and Philosophy Presented to Hans Dieter Betz on his 70th Birthday* (ed. A. Y. Collins and M. M. Mitchell; Tübingen: Mohr, 2001), 321–32. The rhetorical form and similarity to Theophilus seem to give the fragment to Melito.

105. See Hall, *Melito of Sardis*, xlix.

106. Perler, *Méliton de Sardes,* 128–29.

107. Irenaeus, *Heresies* 1, preface.

108. Ibid., 1.13.3.

109. Ibid., 1.15.6.

110. Ibid., 3.17.4.

111. Ibid., 3.23.3.

112. Ibid., 4.4.1.

113. Ibid., 4.27.1.

114. Ibid., 4.27.2.

115. Ibid., 4.30.3.

116. Marcion believed that the Old Testament worthies in Hades refused to accept Christ (Irenaeus, *Heresies* 1.27.3).

117. Irenaeus, *Heresies* 4.31.1.

118. Ibid., 4.41.2.

119. Ibid., 5.5.1.

120. Ibid., 5.17.4.

121. Ibid., 5.30.1.

122. Melito mentions Sagaris as martyr in Fragment 4.

123. Feast of unleavened bread called *Pascha*: Luke 22:1; Josephus, *Antiquities* 14.21.

124. Eusebius, *Church History* 5.24.2–8.

125. Ibid., 5.16.3.

126. W. M. Ramsay, *The Cities and Bishoprics of Phrygia* 2 (Oxford: Clarendon Press, 1897), 657; cf. G. Lüdtke and T. Nissen, *Abercii Titulus Sepulcralis* (Leipzig: Teubner, 1910).

127. *On Illustrious Men* 40. Tertullian's work discussed such Asian Christians as Melito of Sardis.

128. In May 2002 William Tabernee's discovery of these villages was announced at a meeting of the North American Patristics Society. See chap. 25, Oracle 11.

129. R. E. Heine, *The Montanist Oracles and Testimonia*. NAPS Patristic Monograph Series, 14. Macon, Ga.: Mercer University Press, 1989, 25, following K. Lake (translation in LCL), emends the name to "Pompinus." This seems to replace one unknown by another.

130. Eusebius, *Church History* 5.18.

131. Unfortunately Gratus cannot be identified.

132. Eusebius, *Church History* 5.16.2–17.4.

133. Heine, *The Montanist Oracles*, 2–7.

134. Epiphanius, *Heresies* 48.11.1.

135. Ibid., 48.11.9; cf. Tertullian, *Against Marcion* 4.22.11, also based on Isa. 63:9 ("It was no envoy, no angel, but he himself that delivered them").

136. Ibid., 48.4.1.

137. Ibid., 48.10.3.

138. Eusebius, *Church History* 5.16.17.

139. Epiphanius, *Heresies* 48.2.4.

140. Ibid., 48.12.4.

141. Ibid., 48.13.1 (cf. 13.7).

142. Tertullian, *On the Resurrection of the Flesh* 11.2.

143. Tertullian, *Exhortation to Chastity* 10.5.

144. Epiphanius, *Heresies* 49.1.3.

145. Tertullian, *On Chastity* 21.7.

146. Tertullian, *On Flight* 9.4.

147. Ibid.; cf. *On the Soul* 55.5.

148. Cf. A. D. Nock, "Soter and Euergetes," S. E. Johnson, ed., *The Joy of Study: Papers on New Testament and Related Subjects Presented to Honor Frederick Clifton Grant* (New York: Macmillan Co., 1951), 127–48 (137, n. 35).

149. Eusebius, *Church History* 4.3.2. On Quadratus, Grant, *Greek Apologists*, 35–36.

150. Eusebius, *Church History* 4.23; also 2.25.8; 3.4.10.

151. Nautin, *Lettres et écrivains chrétiens des iie et iiie siècles* (Paris: Cerf, 1961), 13–32; also in Encyclopedia of the Early Church (1992), 238.

152. When Origen contrasted the *ecclesiae* of cities with those of churches he had their behavior in mind, not their structure (*Against Celsus* 3.29–30).

153. R. Cagnat, *Inscriptiones Graecae ad Res Romanas pertinentes* 3 (Paris: Leroux, 1906), 88. *ILS* 5883 names Gaius Julius Aquila as an earlier high priest of "the heavenly god Augustus" at Amastris.

154. Lucian, *Alexander* 25, cited by Cagnat.

155. Strabo describes Amastris briefly (12.3.10, 544–45).

156. Basil, *On the Holy Spirit* (SC 17 bis, 511–13), cited by H. Crouzel, *Grégoire le Thaumaturge Remerciement à Origène* (SC 148, 26).

157. Pliny, *Epistles* 10.96.6. Note that *Epistles* 90–91 deal with Sinope; 92–93 with Amisus; and 98–99 with Amastris, all fairly close together.

158. Eusebius, *Church History* 4.23.10.

159. Ibid., 2.25.8. The picture is obviously based on Clement's "good apostles" (1 Clement 5.3–7).

160. Ibid., 4.23.11.

161. Cf. Matt. 13:25; W. C. van Unnik, "De la règle Μήτε προσθεῖναι μήτε αφελεῖν dans l'histoire du Canon," *Vigiliae Christianae* 3 (1949), 1–36.

162. Eusebius, *Church History* 4.23.12.

163. Ibid., 4.23.13.

164. "The list here, which gives only six of the martyrs instead of the twelve who are executed, seems to have been accidentally shortened in the manuscripts." H. Musurillo, *The Acts of the Christian Martyrs* (Oxford: Clarendon Press, 1972), 87 n.4.

165. Irenaeus also wrote the letter to the churches of Asia and Phrygia (Eusebius, *Church History* 5.1–4), according to Nautin, *Lettres et écrivains chrétiens,* 54–61.

166. Eusebius, *Church History* 5.20.4–8.

167. Ibid., 5.24.12–13.

168. Ibid., 5.24.14–17.

169. R. Knopf, G. Krüger, and G. Ruhbach, *Ausgewählte Märtyrerakten* (Tübingen: Mohr, 1965), 125–26, 137.

170. The MS reads "the bath of myrtle" (μυρτίνου); Recension B reads "of a certain Martin son of Timiotinus"; Cavalieri suggested "of Tiberine" (Τιβυρτίνου) (Musurillo, 48 note).

171. The inscription is not *ILS* 3474 ("in insula Tiberina . . . nunc in Vaticano") but *ILS* 3472 (slightly misread). See chapter 31 below and my photograph in *Greek Apologists,* 46. The apocryphal *Acts of Peter* (c.10, 57 Lipsius) tell of a purely apocryphal inscription dedicated *SIMONI IUVENI DEO* ('to Simon the young god"; note that the goddess Iuventas had a place on the Capitoline [G. Wissowa, *Religion und Kultus der Römer* (3d ed., Munich: Beck, 1912), 135–36]).

172. For Gittae see M. Avi-Yonah, *Gazetteer of Roman Palestine* (Jerusalem: Hebrew University, QEDEM 5, 1976), 46–47; for Capparetaea, ibid., 47 (Capahar-, 46–47; Kefar-, 71–73).

173. Justin, *Apology* 1.26.

174. See Wissowa, *Religion und Kultus,* 129–33.

175. Augustine, *City of God* 18.19 (partly from Varro?).

176. Tertullian, *Apology* 13.9.

177. Clement, *Miscellanies* 7.106.4; Hippolytus, *Refutation* 7.10.1.

178. Clement, *Miscellanies* 4.81–83 ("from the 23rd book of the *Exegetics*").

179. Ibid., 4.86.1.

180. Origen, *Romans Commentary* 5.1.

181. Clement, *Miscellanies* 2.113.4–114.1.

182. Aristotle, *On Pythagorean Matters,* Frag. 3 (W. D. Ross, *Aristotelis Fragmenta Selecta* [Oxford: Clarendon Press, 1955], 133).

183. Clement, *Miscellanies* 6.53.3–5. For Pherecydes, H. Diels and W. Kranz, *Die Fragmente der Vorsokratiker* (6th ed., Berlin: Weidmann, 1951), 1.47 (7 B 2).

184. This paraphrases Matthew: "There are eunuchs who were born so from their mother's womb and there are eunuchs who were eunuchized by men and there are eunuchs who eunuchize themselves for the kingdom of heaven."

185. Clement, *Miscellanies* 3.1–3.

186. Hippolytus, *Refutation* 6.42.2.

187. Clement, *Miscellanies* 2.36.2–4.

188. Cf. Plato, *Republic* 560A.

189. Clement, *Miscellanies* 2.114.3–6.

190. Ibid., 3.59.3.

191. Ibid., 4.89.1–3.

192. Ibid., 4.89.6–90.1.

193. Ibid., 6.52.3–4.

194. Hippolytus, *Refutation* 6.37.7.

195. G. Quispel, *Ptolémée Lettre à Flora* (SC 29 bis; Paris: Cerf, 1949).

196. R. M. Grant, "Notes on Gnosis," *Vigiliae christianae* 11 (1957): 145–51 (147–48); cf. Johannes Lydus, *On the Months* 4.73.

197. This is close to Valentinian terminology for the God of the Old Testament (Quispel, *Ptolémée Lettre*, 96).

198. Epiphanius, *Heresies* 33.3–7.

199. Irenaeus, *Heresies* 1.8.5.

200. Origen, *John Commentary* 2.14.

201. Ibid., 2.21.

202. Ibid., 6.3.

203. Ibid., 6.15. In Origen's view Heracleon had missed a subtle distinction between "prophet" and "the prophet."

204. Ibid., 6.20–21.

205. Ibid., 6.23.

206. Ibid., 6.30.

207. Ibid., 6.39.

208. Ibid., 6.40. Origen himself, with others, read "Bethabara"; still others, "Betharaba."

209. Ibid., 6.60.

210. Ibid., 10.11. Compare Mark 6:5.

211. Ibid., 10.19.

212. Ibid., 10.33.

213. Ibid., 10.34.

214. Ibid., 10.37.

215. Ibid., 10.38.

216. Ibid., 13.10.

217. Ibid., 13.11.
218. Ibid., 13.15.
219. Ibid., 13.16.
220. Ibid., 13.17.
221. Ibid., 13.20.
222. Ibid., 13.19.
223. Ibid., 13.25.
224. Ibid., 13.27.
225. Ibid., 13.28.
226. Ibid., 13.31.
227. Ibid., 13.32.
228. Ibid., 13.34.
229. Ibid., 13.35.
230. Ibid., 13.38.
231. Ibid., 13.41.
232. Ibid., 13.44.
233. Ibid., 13.46.
234. Ibid., 13.49.
235. Ibid., 13.50.
236. Ibid., 13.51.
237. Ibid., 13.52.
238. Ibid., 13.53.
239. Ibid., 13.60.
240. Ibid., 19.14.
241. Ibid., 19.19.
242. Ibid., 20.8.
243. Ibid., 20.20.
244. Ibid., 20.23.
245. Ibid., 20.24.
246. Ibid., 20.28.
247. Ibid., 20.38.
248. Clement, *Prophetic Selections* 25.1.
249. Possibly just a Hebraism, in spite of Heracleon's subtle exegesis.
250. Clement, *Miscellanies* 4.71–72.
251. Eusebius, *Church History* 5.13.5–7.
252. Fragments in A. von Harnack, *Marcion: das Evangelium vom fremden Gott* (2d ed., Leipzig: Hinrichs, 1924), 404*–420*. On Apelles see R. M. Grant, *Heresy and Criticism* (Louisville, Ky.: Westminster John Knox Press, 1993), 76–88; E. Junod, "Les attitudes d'Apelles, disciple de Marcion, à l'égard de l'Ancien Testament," *Augustinianum* 22 (1982): 113–33 (124).
253. From Origen, *Homilies on Genesis* 2.2. On antecedents see E. Stein, "Alttestamentliche Bibelkritik in der späthellenistischen Literatur," *Collectanea theologica* (Lwow, 1935), 18.
254. Ambrose, *On Paradise* 5.28, from "Apelles in the 38th book."
255. Ibid., 6.30.
256. Ibid., 6.31.
257. Ibid., 6.32.
258. Ibid., 7.35.

259. Ibid., 8.38.

260. Ibid., 8.40.

261. Ibid., 8.41.

262. Epiphanius, *Heresies* 44.1.4–6.

263. Anastasius of Sinai, *Anagogical Contemplations On the Six Days' Work* (PG 89.1013C–1014C); "Irenaeus," Greek Fragment 14 (W. W. Harvey, *Sancti Irenaei*, etc. [Cambridge: Cambridge University Press, 1855], 2.483–86, after Massuet).

264. Eusebius, *Church History* 2.25.7.

265. Ibid., 3.28.2.

266. Ibid., 3.31.4.

267. Ibid., 6.20.3.

268. Epiphanius, *Heresies* 51.3.2–6; cf. 51.18.1 (false), 6 (not canonical).

269. Ibid., 51.4.5; cf. 51.18.

270. Ibid., 51.6.14 (Matthew but not Mark).

271. Ibid., 51.17.11.

272. Ibid., 51.22.1.

273. Consul with Poppaeus Sabinus in 9 A.D. (Vettulenus Pompeianus was consul in 136). These data are obviously worthless.

274. Epiphanius, *Heresies* 51.29.2–3.

275. Ibid., 51.32.2.

276. Ibid., 51.33.1.

277. Ibid., 51.34.1–2.

278. Dionysius bar Salibi, *In Apocalypsim Actus et Epistulas Catholicas. Interpretatus est I. Sedlacek*, Corpus scriptorum christianorum orientalium, Series Secunda, 101:1.

279. P. de Labriolle, *La crise montaniste* (Paris: Leroux, 1913), 285.

280. Sedlacek, op. cit., 8–10.

281. Ibid., p.19.

282. Greek letter a=1; b=2; x=60; r=100; s=200.

283. An excessively literal reading of Mark 15:21–24.

284. It is enough for us too that "the whole heresy" was condemned, for nothing else is reliably known about them.

285. Bracketed by Kroymann, CCL 1, 1406.

286. a=1, e=5, i=10, p=80, r=100, s=200, t=300.

287. Backwards from the end of the alphabet.

288. Emend to "Zephyrinus" in view of Hippolytus, *Refutation* 9.11.3, or to "Victor," Oehler in CCL 1, 1.1410.

Select Bibliography

Bammel, C. P. H. "Die erste lateinische Rede gegen die Christen," *Zeitschrift für Kirchengeschichte* 104 (1993): 295–311.

Esler, P. F. *The Early Christian World*. 2 vols. London and New York: Routledge & Kegan Paul, 2000.

Grant, R. M. *Gnosticism: An Anthology*. London: Collins, 1963.

———. *Greek Apologists of the Second Century*. Philadelphia: Westminster Press, 1988.

Hall, S. G. *Melito of Sardis On Pascha and Fragments*. Oxford: Clarendon Press, 1979.

Harnack, A. von. *Marcion: das Evangelium vom fremden Gott*. 2d ed. Texte und Untersuchungen 45. Leipzig: Hinrichs, 1924.

Heine, R. E. *The Montanist Oracles and Testimonia*. NAPS Patristic Monograph Series, 14. Macon, Ga.: Mercer University Press, 1989.

Junod, E. "Les attitudes d'Apelles, disciple de Marcion, à l'égard de l'Ancien Testament," *Augustinianum* 22 (1982): 113–33.

Knopf, R., Krüger, G., and Ruhbach, G. *Ausgewählte Märtyrerakten*. Tübingen: Mohr, 1965.

Labriolle, P. de. *La crise montaniste*. Paris: Leroux, 1913.

Lawlor, H. J., and Oulton, J. E. L. *Eusebius: The Ecclesiastical History and The Martyrs of Palestine*. 2 vols. London: SPCK, 1928.

Lohse, B. *Das Passafest der Quartadecimaner*. Gütersloh: Bertelsmann, 1953.

Musurillo, H. *The Acts of the Christian Martyrs*. Oxford: Clarendon Press, 1972.

Perler, O. *Méliton de Sardes. Sur la pâque et fragments*. SC 123. Paris: Cerf, 1966.

Preuschen, E. *Antilegomena. Die Reste der ausserkanonischen Evangelien und urchristlichen Ueberlieferungen*. Giessen: Ricker, 1901.

Quispel, G. *Ptolémée Lettre à Flora*. SC. Paris: Cerf, 1949.

Schoedel, W. R. *Polycarp, Martyrdom of Polycarp, Fragments of Papias*. Camden, N.J.: Thomas Nelson & Sons, 1967.

Sedlacek, I. *Dionysius bar Salibi, In Apocalypsim Actus et Epistulas Catholicas*. Corpus scriptorum christianorum orientalium, Series Secunda, 101. 1910.

Tabbernee, W. "Portals of the Montanist New Jerusalem: The Discovery of Pepouza and Tymion," *Journal of Early Christian Studies* 11 (2003): 87–93.

Torrey, C. C. "James the Just and his Name 'Oblias.'" *Journal of Biblical Literature* 63 (1944): 93–98.

Völker, W. *Quellen zur Geschichte der christlichen Gnosis*. Tübingen: Mohr, 1932.

Walzer, R. *Galen on Jews and Christians*. London: Oxford University Press, 1949.

Wilken, R. L. *The Christians as the Romans Saw Them*. New Haven, Conn.: Yale University Press, 1984.

Index of Names

Index of Subjects